Gien Karssen is a storyteller. Although there are many studies about the women in the Bible, I have never read one more practical than *Her Name Is Woman*. Gien makes these biblical women really come alive as you observe their actions and the effects of their lives. She helps you draw out applications that are relevant today. Gien is one of the best trainers I know for young Bible study leaders. She brings the Word of God to bear upon situations in day-to-day living. My prayer is that this book will work as a seed that brings forth much fruit.

CORRIE TEN BOOM
Author of *The Hiding Place*

All my life I have read about the women of the Bible, learning much from them even though they were somewhat vague, historic characters. In this book, these same characters have suddenly come alive. Because of Gien's careful research, sanctified imagination, and skill as a writer, I found myself understanding these women and their situations in a new way. Knowing more about the customs of their day helps us understand better why they acted as they did. It is interesting to note that God's women, down through the centuries, have enjoyed a freedom the world finds difficult to understand— the freedom to be and to do that which God intended. You will find this book both interesting and enlightening.

RUTH BELL GRAHAM
Author of *Footprints of a Pilgrim*

Learners

lessons from women of striving and grace

HER NAME IS WOMAN BIBLE STUDY

Gien Karssen

NAVPRESS

A NavPress resource published in alliance
with Tyndale House Publishers, Inc.

NavPress ®

NavPress is the publishing ministry of The Navigators, an international Christian organization and leader in personal spiritual development. NavPress is committed to helping people grow spiritually and enjoy lives of meaning and hope through personal and group resources that are biblically rooted, culturally relevant, and highly practical.

For more information, visit www.NavPress.com.

The Team:
    Don Pape, Publisher
    Caitlyn Carlson, Acquisitions Editor

Cover design by Jacqueline L. Nuñez

Cover photograph of woman copyright © Niko Guido/Getty Images. All rights reserved.

Cover illustration of wreath copyright © MarushaBelle/Shutterstock. All rights reserved.

Library of Congress Cataloging-in-Publication Data

Karssen, Gien.
    Her name is woman : learners : lessons from women of striving and grace / Gien Karssen.
      pages cm
      ISBN 978-1-63146-420-1
  1. Women in the Bible—Biography.   2. Bible—Biography.   I. Title.
      BS575.K36933 2015
      220.9'2082—dc23   2015012053

Printed in the United States of America

21	20	19	18	17	16	15
7	6	5	4	3	2	1

I dedicate this book to my many friends within The Navigators organization around the world. The plan to write the Her Name Is Woman series began to ripen through my global contact with young women. I saw in them the same fascination for the lives of women in the Bible that I have.

I further remember many, many others, men and women, who through their teachings, example, and friendship have made an indelible impression upon my life. I think of the first Navigator I met years ago—Dawson Trotman, the founder of the organization—and of the many young people who have found a personal faith in Jesus Christ through the ministry of The Navigators recently.

They all have three things in common: a great love for God, a deep reverence for His Word, and a passion to share their lives with others. Two words are applicable to almost all of them: realism and enthusiasm.

Through my fellowship with The Navigators, the intense desire to be a woman after the heart of God grew within me. For this reason the women in this book are not just people of a dim, distant past, but real people, living and sparkling. It is my desire that every person who reads this book will be challenged in the same way to live wholeheartedly for God. It is my desire that they be encouraged and built up. And, at the same time, I trust this book will prove to be an instrument in their hands whereby they can help others.

Contents

Foreword

RALPH WALDO EMERSON said, "I have never met a man who was not my superior in some particular." In other words, each person we meet has the potential to teach us something new if we are willing to look for the lesson in every conversation and situation. There is no end to the opportunities to grow in our knowledge, wisdom, and understanding, and the Scriptures command it. We are instructed to learn the commandments, to learn to love the Lord, to learn to fear the Lord, to learn to do right and seek justice, to learn the secret of being content, and to learn to control our bodies. Hebrews even tells us that Jesus Himself "learned obedience" (Hebrews 5:8). That's just a sampling of the many exhortations to be lifelong learners that we find in the Scriptures.

When we learn something new about God, it opens up a window of how much more we need to learn. We don't engage in learning because we are unwise but because we are wise. It's not about making ourselves better but about getting to know God better.

Like Emerson, we can learn much from the women in the

Story of God, even from those whose lives were the messiest and most broken. Eve learned identity and purpose, Sarah learned of God's providence and sovereignty, and Rebekah learned the tragic results of not waiting on the perfect timing of God. Reading Bathsheba's story, we are perplexed by the extravagant grace of God. When reading the story of the widow of Zarephath, we learn that faith is not primarily a mindset but a series of actions. The stories of Tamar and Naomi show us that redemption is always found—even if it is waiting far ahead of us in the future. These women teach us to hold on to faith when it seems as though faith has let go of us, and they teach us that we must develop the kind of faith that stands the test of life.

Jesus taught his disciples with stories, and Gien Karssen does the same. She tackles familiar stories but zooms in on the characters so we see them and understand them more clearly. She shines a spotlight on the tension, the choices, the revelations, the triumphs and failures, and the thrills and disappointments that each woman encounters. She gives us a window to see how they responded when God showed up the way they expected and how they reacted when He seemed to remain hidden and silent. We can take a front-row seat to learn from their successes and their mistakes. Although separated by thousands of years and thousands of miles, these women are not that different from us. And from them, we can learn valuable lessons.

Heather Zempel, discipleship pastor and
author of Amazed and Confused

How to Use This Study

Do you long for a meaningful life? Do you want to become whole and fulfilled? These inborn, inner urges originate from the commission God gave woman at her creation. He expects woman, an equal partner with man, to be willing to step into her calling. The spiritual side of a woman is extremely important.

The women in this book are not fictional. They are real. They lived in history and, in their desires and problems, in their hopes and ambitions, are living among us today. Though the Bible doesn't share the full extent of their stories, I imaginatively explore what these women may have been doing and feeling in the time and place in which God placed them, in hopes that you will connect with their journeys even further.

As you learn about each of the women throughout the Her Name Is Woman series, the central question you must ask is, What place does God have in her life? The answer to this question decides the extent of every woman's happiness, usefulness, and motivation to keep moving forward. If God is absent, or if He is not given His rightful place, then life is without true purpose—without perspective.

As you read this book, join with these women of the Bible to consider your attitude toward God. And I hope that as you get acquainted with these women, you will make a fresh or renewed start in getting to know the Word of God.

I trust that meeting these women will turn out to be an unexpected gift for you and that you will resonate deeply with their experiences—and I pray that they will show you the way to a richer and happier life with God and other people.

AS YOU BEGIN

You may approach this book in one of two ways. First, just read it. The stories are intended to draw you deeply into the life of each woman in these pages. But be sure to include the Bible passages referenced at the beginning of each chapter in your reading. They are an important part of the book and are necessary for understanding the chapter. Second, you may wish to discuss the book in a small group. Considering the subjects and questions with some other people will add depth and greater insight to your study of these women.

Scripture references at the bottom of many pages will help you dig deeper into the Bible's wealth of truth and wisdom. You may answer the questions throughout each chapter personally or discuss them with your group. You may also conduct topical studies of these women or research accompanying themes.

Whatever your direction might be, this study will become richer as you discuss these women with others, especially after your own individual preparation. Whether you do this study on your own or with others, be sure to use a journal so you may record your thoughts on the questions and any other things God impresses on your heart through the course of this study.

SUGGESTIONS FOR BIBLE STUDY GROUPS

1. Start with a small group—usually with a minimum of six and a maximum of ten people. This way your group will be large enough for an interesting discussion but small enough for each member to participate. As your number increases, start a second group.

2. Before you start the group, decide how often you want to meet. Many people may hesitate to give themselves to something new for an indefinite period of time. There are twelve chapters in each book of the Her Name Is Woman series, so they may easily be used as twelve-week studies. However, these books can just as easily work as six-week studies (two chapters a week). Some chapters are longer and will take more time to work through, while others are short enough to be combined into a two-part lesson. Please note that the number of questions varies depending on the length of the lesson. Discuss what process will work best for your group.

3. Remember that a Bible study group should discuss the Bible. While many of the questions within this book

are designed to help women examine their individual faith journeys, Scripture informs every piece of the study and should be referenced as an integral part of the discussion. Each participant should prepare her study at home beforehand so each member may share her personal findings.

4. Stress the necessity of applying the lessons learned, and help one another in doing this. There is a far greater need for spiritual growth than for an increase of knowledge. "How can what I learned influence my life?" is a question each participant should ask herself.

5. Determine, before you start, to attend every meeting. Miss only when you absolutely cannot attend. If you can't attend, do the study anyway and make up for it at the next meeting.

6. Consider yourself a member of the group. Feel free to make a contribution. Lack of experience should not keep you from taking part in the discussion. On the other hand, resist the temptation to dominate the group.

SUGGESTIONS FOR LEADERS OF BIBLE STUDY GROUPS

- Be sure that you have given sufficient time to your own Bible study and that you have completed it.
- Come prepared. Make notes of the points you want to stress.

- Begin and end on time. Set the tone by starting promptly at the first meeting.
- Few mountain climbers enjoy being carried to the top. Leave the joy of climbing to the group members. Don't do all the talking. Guide the discussion in such a way that each member of the group can participate.
- Don't allow any one person to dominate the conversation. Gently guide the group so each person may have an opportunity to speak. Sometimes it is necessary to talk privately with an overtalkative person, explaining the necessity of group participation. While some women may prefer to remain quiet, give them the opportunity to participate by asking them specific questions.
- Use the questions throughout each chapter as a jumping-off point, but feel the freedom to focus on issues that seem to particularly resonate with your group. However, don't allow the group to get too off topic. If a particular question becomes too time consuming or detracts from the overall study, redirect the conversation back to the main study. Getting back on track when the subject begins to wander can be done by saying, "Perhaps we could discuss this further after the study," or "Let's return to the main focus of the study."
- At the beginning of each session, open with prayer. Pray that Christ will speak to each person present by His Word. At the end of each session, pray for yourself and for each member of the group. Pray that the Holy Spirit will make you sensitive to the needs of others.

1
EVE

The Mother of All Living

The woman was made of a rib out of the side of Adam;
not made out of his head to rule over him, nor out of his feet
to be trampled upon by him, but out of his side to be equal
with him, under his arm to be protected, and near his heart
to be beloved.

MATTHEW HENRY, *A COMMENTARY ON THE WHOLE BIBLE*

READ

Genesis 1:27-28; Genesis 2:18, 20-25; Genesis 3:1-20

• • •

EVE WAS CAPTIVATED BY ALL SHE SAW—everything around her
was perfect. The nature she saw was wondrous and refresh-
ing. The air she breathed was pure and unspoiled. The water
she drank was clear and sparkling. Every animal lived harmo-
niously with all others.

Her marriage was perfect—her fellowship with God and
her husband were a daily joy. Eve had everything anyone
could desire.

Then one day a voice in the garden asked her, "Did

God tell you that you should not eat the fruit of any tree in the garden?"

Why, she wondered, *haven't I ever noticed the special beauty of the tree that stands in the middle of the garden? And why does my entire happiness suddenly seem to depend on eating its fruit? Eating something so desirable can only be good . . .*

Reflect on a time when you felt as though your happiness depended on something other than God alone. How did you respond to the temptations involved?

She didn't notice that she was being deceived—that God's Word had been twisted—that God's love was being doubted.

Eve didn't know that the one speaking to her was Satan in disguise.[1] He was and had been a liar and a murderer from the beginning,[2] desiring to deceive people.[3] He didn't quote God precisely, but used his own words.[4]

His attack on God's Word should have warned her not to listen to him. She could still have escaped at this phase of her temptation.[5] For although she was on dangerous ground, she had been created with a will that was capable of withstanding the tempter. She didn't have to give Satan the opportunity to deceive her by listening to him.[6] She had a choice. But

---

[1] 2 Corinthians 11:14; Revelation 20:2
[2] John 8:44
[3] 1 Peter 5:8 ·
[4] Genesis 2:16-17
[5] James 4:7
[6] Ephesians 4:27

unfortunately, she listened to him. Even worse, she answered him. This marked the beginning of her fall.

Like Satan, Eve also twisted the words of God. She added, "And you must not touch it . . ." to what God said, although God had not said anything about touching. Then she weakened His stress on death by omitting the word *certainly*.

---

*Have you ever been guilty of
softening or changing God's words
to align with your personal desires?
What does such an action indicate about
a person's heart and motivations?*

Satan's first blow was successful. Eve was willing to listen to him, to linger with him. This increased his boldness. He blatantly called God a liar. He portrayed God as Someone who wanted to subdue humans and curtail their happiness, since He had the power to do so.

"Die?" he railed. "You won't die at all. You will be happier than you ever dreamed. You will be like God." He continued to tempt her, drawing her toward independence. His call to disobedience was fatal to Eve. Her resistance had been broken when she took time to argue with Satan. She stretched forward and took the fruit that her heart desired.

By then, the evil could not be stopped. She had become so entangled in the nets of the deceiver that she could not escape. She ate the fruit. But that was not the end of the matter. The woman who was deceived in turn became a deceiver. Eve entangled her husband in her sin. Without protest he accepted the fruit from her and ate it.

**Reflect on a time when a sin choice
in your life impacted someone else.
What did you learn from that experience?**

At that moment her entire life changed.

In the beginning, the creation God had made was ideal. It was so perfect that He was satisfied with it Himself[7] and stressed this fact after every deed of creation.

Yet something was missing. "It is not good for a man to be alone. I will make him a helper," said the Lord God. After both man and woman were created, God's work was complete and "very good."[8]

Eve was a creature carved by the hand of God. She was created equal to her husband. Their only difference was sex. She was unique.

As a human being, she, like Adam, was gifted with reason and understanding. Therefore, she was his partner in conversation. And like him she had a personal relationship with and was expected to be obedient to her Creator. God made Eve, along with Adam, accountable for executing the same tasks.

[7] Genesis 1:10, 12, 18, 21, 25
[8] Genesis 1:31

In her own specific way, she was to help fill and subdue the earth. She had a unique relationship with her husband. She shared her life with him. She completed him. Her physical structure made her fit him, so that together they could execute God's command to multiply.

Although completed after Adam, Eve was certainly not an "afterthought." She was as much a part of God's original plan as Adam was. She couldn't function without him, and he could not do without her.[9]

As husband and wife, Adam and Eve formed a new nucleus: a couple. This couple was characterized by its own personality. It was not the sum of two individuals; it was its own new entity. It is God's plan that the marriage partners should live together in complete harmony—that they feel at ease with each other, one in a bond maintained by mutual love and respect.[10]

In the wake of her conversation with Satan, Eve realized how bitterly she had been deceived. She first noticed this in her relationship to Adam. They had always been at ease with each other, as God had created them to be. But now they were suddenly shy and defenseless. The protection of their innocence was gone. They discovered they could not have a free and easy relationship. They began to hide things from each other. They discovered that they not only stood naked to each other—they were naked before God! Their purity was gone. Their sinless nature had been destroyed.

[9] 1 Corinthians 11:11-12
[10] Ephesians 5:21

Their intimate relationship with God was broken. Instead of becoming like Him as Satan had promised, they became afraid of Him and fled from Him.

What specific recurring issues do you see in your relationships that are an effect of the fall? How is Christ's sacrifice for your sin redeeming those issues?

Then God entered this devastating situation. He took the initiative to look for them. How lovingly He greeted them. He started with a question, not an accusation. He gave them a chance to acknowledge their sin, but they failed to see their opportunity. He first held Adam responsible for his role.[11] Though Adam had been present, he did not stop Eve from committing the sin. In fact, he joined her. And then he blamed her. "The woman You gave me did it." Adam almost sounded as if he blamed God for giving Eve to him.

Eve passed the guilt on to someone else too. She blamed the serpent, although if she had been honest with herself, she would have had to admit that she had voluntarily accepted his offer. It was true, he had misled her, but she had sinned of her own free will. She had failed the test offered to her as a human being to obey God voluntarily out of love.

[11] Romans 5:12, 14

In what part of your life are you not taking responsibility for your own sin? Have you ever blamed others for choices that are ultimately yours? How can you change your perspective and response to these areas?

The judgment of God that followed revealed to her the catastrophic impact of her deed. Not only the beautiful Garden of Eden, but the entire world, was cursed. The soil, once without weeds, would now produce thorns and thistles. The animals were cursed. The tranquility of the animal kingdom over which Adam and Eve had ruled together was marred. The wolf and lamb would no longer eat peacefully together. The stronger would rule the weaker. The beautiful paradise in which they could have lived happily forever had, with one quick blow, become a lost paradise. They were ordered to leave quickly, so they wouldn't eat from the tree of life and thus be forced to live forever as sinful people.[12]

Eve, who had completed God's creation and who was the last link in the chain of happiness on earth, had thrown this happiness away by her disobedience.

Her joy of motherhood would be tempered by pain and trouble. The sting of lordship would now affect her relationship with her husband. He would now rule over her because of sin.

---
[12] Genesis 3:22-23

And though Adam and Eve did not die instantly after their sin in the Garden, the institution of death was a result. In a second they had become mortal human beings, subject to death.

But far worse than natural death was spiritual death, the vacuum of separation from God.[13] This, most of all, Eve painfully experienced in her innermost self.

If you are a follower of Christ, you are no longer separated from God. However, often in our sin we still hide from God, though He longs to be close to us. Have you experienced relational distance because of sin? What did you learn from that experience?

Eve was lonely and had a difficult time during childbirth. Being the first woman on earth she had no mother, no sister, no friend who could share her feelings. There was no one to go to for advice, no other woman who could help her with the delivery. And what a strange experience, to become a mother when you have never been a child yourself. What do you do with a child? In these trying circumstances it is no wonder that Eve fell back on God. "With the help of the LORD I have brought forth a man,"[14] she said as she smiled at her baby, Cain.

She and Adam were not the only ones to be punished for

[13] Genesis 2:17; Ephesians 2:1
[14] Genesis 4:1

sinning against God. Satan's punishment was far greater. He was told of his destruction, by Someone named Immanuel, who would be born of Eve's offspring.[15] Was she hoping, was she expecting, that the child in her arms was the promised Messiah?

Eve was a living demonstration of faith—faith that one could never sink so deeply so as not to be able to turn back to God. And hope—hope that God would give new possibilities, no matter how great the sin.

_____

Read Romans 5:3-4, and reflect on how God spurs us toward hope. Does God's response toward your sin cause you to hope? Has your hope grown over the course of your walk with Him?

_____

Eve was crushed when Cain killed her second son. She realized that she had brought a sinful man into the world. He was a murderer. The terrible extent of her deed in the garden became even more starkly clear to her. She had passed on death—spiritually and physically—to Adam, and he to every person born.[16] No human would ever again live in innocence, as she once had. Each person born would sin not only by choice, but also because of an inner urging. Everyone would face an unending battle between good and evil. Everyone would be separated from God by sin. There would be no exceptions.

_____

[15] Isaiah 7:14
[16] Romans 3:10-12, 23; 6:23

Again and again Satan appeals to the desires of man, trying to entice him. Sin and death will enter the scene each time we give in to our own desires.[17] In every generation there will be people like Eve who are moved by the desire to have what the eyes see and to satisfy the desires of pride.[18] Satan tries to move every person against God just as he did to Eve. He stirs up rebellion and ingratitude in order to cause men to fall like he fell—from pride.[19]

Even many, many years after Eden, when Jesus Christ has offered us redemption[20] and everyone who personally believes in Him again has access to God,[21] the best of us will realize that while we want to do good, we are drawn toward evil.[22] Only Jesus Christ—the Announced One—has proven that a man can conquer temptation if he clings to and lives by the Word of God.[23]

Knowledge of God's Word and His desires for us help protect us from temptation. What is one specific practice you can begin this week to expand your knowledge of Scripture?

As a result of Adam and Eve's sin, the tears, mourning, and pain we experience now will continue until a new kingdom.[24]

---

[17] James 1:14-15
[18] 1 John 2:16
[19] Isaiah 14:12-15
[20] 1 John 2:2
[21] John 1:12-13
[22] Romans 7:15-19
[23] Matthew 4:1-11
[24] Revelation 21:1, 4

And until that time, every human will be plagued with sin. Until then, every person is urgently warned not to follow Eve's example.[25] For Eve, the mother of all living, provides a frightening example. She is the woman who admitted sin into the world when she allowed Satan to make her doubt God's Word and His love. But may we also learn from her faith that God can redeem the darkest of stories.

---

[25] 2 Corinthians 11:3

2
SARAH

The Princess Whose Name Is Recorded with Honor

Faith is confidence, reliance, trust. It is the sixth sense which enables us to apprehend the invisible but real spiritual realm. Within this realm its dealings are directly with God.

J. OSWALD SANDERS, *MIGHTY FAITH*

READ

Genesis 18:1-15; Genesis 21:1-13; Hebrews 11:11;
1 Peter 3:6

• • •

THE SCENE IS HEBRON, two thousand years before Christ.

Sarah laughs, but not because she is happy. She laughs because of what she has heard—that she, a woman of eighty-nine, will give birth to a child! A son. Impossible!

She and her husband are too old for a baby. It is biologically impossible that she could bring forth a child, although they have been waiting for many years. They were convinced that God Himself had promised them a son twenty-five years ago, but the promise was not fulfilled. They must have been mistaken. Sarah reflected back on those years . . .

They had lived in Ur, a center of culture and commerce in South Mesopotamia. Though Ur had passed its peak in history, it still provided a flourishing existence. Its craftsmen were surpassed only by those of Egypt. The ships in the harbor brought goods from the East in exchange for locally grown grains. Many citizens were rich and lived in spacious homes.

She and Abraham had enjoyed their time there, living among relatives and friends. But one day their lives were radically changed. Abraham's father, Terah, decided to move them out of Ur. They suddenly became nomads instead of citizens of a wealthy, comfortable city. As with most women, she hadn't found it easy to leave her home and loved ones behind to face an unknown future.

For months they had traveled, moving slowly across the land because of their animals. Finally, they had arrived in Harran, six hundred miles northwest. They stayed there a long time, and life again became a little more comfortable, though not as luxurious as it had been in Ur. However, it was considerably better than their previous roving existence.

But then God had appeared to Abraham.[1] His appearance was so glorious[2] that it had removed all doubt as to who He was. This was the true God, not the moon god Sin, whom Abraham's forefathers had worshiped.[3]

God had ordered Abraham to leave his land and relatives

---

[1] Genesis 11:31–12:5
[2] Acts 7:2-3
[3] Joshua 24:2

to go to a country that He would point out. The order had been linked with a promise: "I will make you into a great nation, and I will bless you; I will make your name great, and you will be a blessing. I will bless those who bless you, and whoever curses you I will curse; and all peoples on earth will be blessed through you."[4]

Reflect on a time when God asked you to make a major life change—a move, a job change, a marriage, etc. How did you actively trust Him during that time? What did He teach you through the experience?

Abraham had obeyed immediately. And there had been another move. This time to the southwest. A little more of Sarah's security had crumbled away. Terah, their father, had died. She was Abraham's half sister. But that wasn't unusual—since opportunities to marry in those days were so limited, one often had to look for a partner within the innermost family circle. With their father's death and the absence of those relatives who stayed behind in Harran,[5] life had become even lonelier. Only Lot, a cousin, traveled with them. Sarah had to trust her husband and the God who had spoken to him.

[4] Genesis 12:2-3
[5] Genesis 24:4, 10; 27:43

―――――――

*Have you ever felt like God was chipping away
everything in which you placed your security?
What did you struggle with in the midst of
that? What did you learn about the things
on which you built your foundation?*

―――――――

Despite their losses, two things had remained unchanged. First, they had continued to believe the promises of God. They felt they would have the child, even though they were getting older—Abraham was seventy-five and Sarah was sixty-five. Second, they had continued to experience a lasting respect and love toward each other.

It hadn't all been easy. Like Abraham, Sarah had a strong personality with a well-developed character. She had done her best to adjust herself to the situation and to trust her husband. She definitely had a mind of her own, yet she had been able to follow him because of an inner freedom.

―――――――

*When have you observed the correlation between
trust and inner freedom in your life? What
Scripture comes to mind to confirm this truth?*

―――――――

Yes, as she reflected on it, her relationship with her husband was determined by her relationship with God. Her trust in God had made her a faithful, strong woman, enabling her to stand in life undaunted and steadfast, living in harmony with her husband.[6]

She respected and honored Abraham, and he in turn respected her, listened to her advice, and honored her with his friendship. They were friends as well as lovers, discussing matters of mutual, daily concern. Since they were open to God and to each other, their marriage and spiritual lives were strong.

Time had passed, but they still had no child. Meanwhile, they had arrived at Shechem, where God appeared to Abraham again and said, "To your offspring I will give this land."[7]

At last they had reached their destination. And they had still hoped for the promised child. In gratitude Abraham had built an altar to God. But because a severe famine came upon the land, Abraham had moved southward in order to get food for his family and animals. He had done this on his own, without asking God's counsel. They had gone to Egypt. Had they gone in a direction not pleasing to God?[8]

Have you ever "gone in a direction" without seeking God? What was the result? How did it impact your relationship with Him?

It had not been easy in Egypt. Because Sarah was beautiful, Abraham had feared for his life, feeling that the Egyptians

[6] 1 Peter 3:1-7
[7] Genesis 12:6-7
[8] Exodus 33:14-15

would kill him in order to get her. So Abraham had said to her, "Please tell them you are my sister so that they won't try to kill me."[9] He had taken refuge in a lie, because of fear. Yet he was a man who had trusted God for years. *What about his love for me?* Sarah had wondered.

It was true that in the beginning of their wanderings they had agreed to use this tactic. They had quieted their consciences with the fact that actually it wasn't a lie.[10] Theoretically this had sounded acceptable, but in practice she had felt betrayed.

Just as Abraham had expected, her beauty had been noticed. She ended up in the pharaoh's harem. Abraham's fear of dying had not merely endangered her purity; she had felt he acted in disregard to the promise of their child.

But the God in whom she had trusted intervened. Through torment and great plagues, God had made the situation clear to the heathen king.[11] She had lost some confidence in her husband as a result of the whole affair. Momentarily, he had left his pedestal. A bit more of her security had crumbled away.

They had then returned to the land God had promised them, bringing with them a young Egyptian slave girl, Hagar. As the years passed without the promised child, Abraham had wondered if perhaps an adopted son would be God's solution. Perhaps the son should be Eliezer, the most important man in his household.[12]

---

[9] Genesis 12:13, author's paraphrase
[10] Genesis 20:12-13
[11] Genesis 12:10-20
[12] Genesis 15:1-4

But that was not God's plan. God had promised that a son conceived by Sarah would be the heir. The promise of a descendant remained unchanged and was confirmed by an oath.[13] Though God had repeated His promises, He had been slow in fulfilling them.

---

*What is a situation in your life in which
you feel God has been slow to act?
What has He taught you during this time?*

Sarah knew from experience that to live a life of faith she was asked not only to abstain from human security, but also to be patient. Faith and patience went together. They couldn't be purchased easily like merchandise but had to be learned through the difficult school of life. They needed exercise[14] and were proven by actual deeds. She and Abraham had had to learn that faith is to be anchored in the solid ground of God's promises and not in the quicksand of human possibilities.

But she had become impatient. Taking into account that her childbearing years were past, she had suggested that Abraham take Hagar, the Egyptian maid, as a concubine.[15] Outwardly, she had adapted herself to the customs of the time. After all, such things occurred frequently. Probably she could have legally defended her action by referring to her wedding contract, in which she had promised her

13 Genesis 15:5-21
14 Hebrews 6:13-15
15 Genesis 16

husband a son. But what she had done was wrong because it lacked faith.

Her self-denial had led her to great sacrifice. She could have offered the excuse that God had not said that the promised son would be her own child. But had she made an unnecessary sacrifice because she wanted desperately to see God's promise fulfilled at any cost and at her chosen time? The long time of waiting, ten years by then, had been nearly unbearable. Her real problem probably hadn't been that her patience wore thin but that she had sought the solution herself. She had taken her lot into her own hands and had paid heavily for it.

Think of a time when you tried to take a situation into your own hands and impose your own solution separate from God's leading. Were there consequences? If so, what did you learn from them?

What had moved Abraham to listen to her? That still was not clear. But like Adam before him, he had plucked the bitter fruit of listening to the wrong suggestion of his wife.[16] Oh, why had he listened?

The consequences were evident almost immediately. The sin of unbelief and impatience had begun bearing fruit even

[16] Genesis 3:17

before the child was long in Hagar's womb. The patriarchal home had been torn by discontent and lack of peace. Hagar had developed a feeling of superiority.

Sarah had forgotten that she had taken the initiative in the unhappy plan. Because she had departed from God, she had neglected to search her own heart or to repent. Instead, she had blamed her husband. She had humiliated Hagar so deeply that, if God had not interceded, the young woman probably would have died. Sarah had degraded herself. She had learned what destructive powers a person can unleash when he or she wanders away from God.

Have you ever caused hurt in a time when you weren't walking closely with the Lord? How did you respond when you realized the impact of your actions?

She had wanted to win time. There was no way to know whether this resulted in actually losing time instead.

One day Abraham was very busy waiting on his guests, who had suddenly come from nowhere and stood before him. During their visit Sarah helped by preparing the meal. When the time came to serve, she had remained in the background, as was the custom in the East.

Her attention was aroused when she heard one of them ask, "Where is your wife, Sarah?" As she walked toward the entrance of the tent, she wondered, *Who are these men? How do they know my name? What else do they know about me?*

Abraham told them, "She is in the tent."

Then came the surprising statement: "I will return to you in a year; and behold Sarah, your wife, shall have a son."

The men were still sitting with their backs toward the tent, and Sarah felt she wouldn't be noticed. She was alone with her thoughts. In her heart she laughed about these words. They were very polite, actually. They were gentlemen. They showed their gratitude for the hospitality by courteously promising the host a son.

Suddenly her musing was over as she was brought abruptly back to reality. Startled, she heard her unspoken thoughts said in words. The man asked, "Why did Sarah laugh, asking, 'How shall I bear a son at my age?'" He followed immediately with the impressive words, "Is there anything too difficult for the Lord?"

The Lord? The Lord?

Then she recognized Him, as Abraham had already recognized Him. Hadn't her husband addressed the three people in the singular with, "My Lord?"

The Lord Himself had descended from heaven to talk to her, to confirm the promise to her personally: "At this time next year I will return, and Sarah shall have a son."

Totally shocked, she denied her lack of faith and said, "I did not laugh." She knew His reply before He made it: "Yes, you did."[17]

---

[17] Genesis 18:10-15, author's paraphrase

Why didn't the Lord address me directly? she wondered. Because it was an Eastern way of life to speak to a woman through her husband? Or did He want to remind Abraham that he, like his wife, had laughed in unbelief? Not too long ago God had repeated the promise of a son to him.[18] But Abraham had also lost hope of ever receiving a son from Sarah. He was satisfied with Ishmael and had begged that he would be acceptable to God.

We often find our satisfaction in things far less than what God has to offer us in our relationship with Him. What is a "lesser thing" that you are holding onto right now? What are three steps you can take this week to release that to God?

For the first time God said explicitly that the son of the promise would be the son of Sarah. As proof of this He had changed their names. Instead of Abram, "exalted father," from now on his name would be Abraham, the "father of a multitude." Sarai was changed to Sarah, meaning "princess." The Lord had not considered it sufficient to tell only Abraham that his time of waiting was coming to an end. He had also come to tell Sarah personally.

The next year, at the time appointed by God, a son was born. The name that Abraham gave him, Isaac, means

---

[18] Genesis 17

"laughing one." As long as they lived, Isaac would remind his parents of the fact that in unbelief they had put a question mark behind his name, which God had changed into an exclamation mark. The results of Sarah's mistake of allowing Hagar to become Abraham's concubine continued to be very serious. Because Ishmael had mocked Isaac at his weaning feast, Sarah urged Abraham to send Hagar and Ishmael away. There was sorrow in Abraham's heart, for he also suffered from his participation in the sin. God told him, however, to listen to Sarah. So he sent the Egyptian away with his child. God loved them too, as history has proven, but there developed a distinct separation between the descendants of Isaac and of Ishmael. Sarah lived only thirty-seven more years after Isaac's birth, so she did not see the misery and sorrow that was released by the descendants of Abraham's two sons.

The Arabs, the descendants of Ishmael, and the Jews, the descendants of Isaac, have become lasting enemies. After many centuries the problems in the Middle East are still awaiting a solution.

How very sad for Sarah that her one deed of impatience had such far-reaching effects and that her memory had to be marred by this. But the Bible doesn't finish her story in a minor key.

The first woman presented in the portrait gallery of the heroes of faith in Hebrews 11 is Sarah. She is recorded with honor because of the faith she did have, not because of her failures.

Her faith, majestically illustrated at the birth of Isaac, grew during her long life. Life had requested many sacrifices from Sarah. She abstained from many things she loved and wanted. She experienced hardships and disappointments— all without murmuring. She was flexible in changing situations. She adjusted herself to her husband. By following Abraham in his call, she allowed him to obey God.

Scientists have discovered that bad emotions can make a person ill. They also say that healthy emotions governed by a sense of happiness, contentment, and an unshaken belief in God can cause physical beauty, good health, and a long life.

Which experiences in Sarah's life
gave her faith a chance to grow?
(Study also Genesis 11:27-32; 12; and 20.)

Could that have been the secret of Sarah's outward beauty and vitality? Peter praises Sarah for her inner beauty and challenges all women to follow her example. For Sarah truly is a princess among women.

3

REBEKAH

A Woman with Great Potential, yet . . .

A wife of noble character who can find? She is worth far more than rubies.

PROVERBS 31:10

READ

Genesis 24:1-28, 58-67

• • •

The Marriage Proposal

IT BEGAN MUCH LIKE A FAIRY TALE. A much-desired bachelor, the only son of a wealthy father and the heir to a massive fortune,[1] was looking for a wife. Even before his birth, God had promised that he would have numerous offspring. God had also said that He would make an everlasting covenant with him and his descendants.[2] Therefore, the mother of these children and grandmother of the children's children needed to be chosen very carefully.

---

[1] Genesis 24:34-36
[2] Genesis 12:2-3; 17:19

Isaac was the young bachelor. His father, Abraham, made all the preparations for the wedding—he even chose the bride. He had sent a man whom he could trust with this delicate commission—probably Eliezer, the steward of his house[3]—to Harran in Mesopotamia, where Abraham had lived earlier. Some of his relatives were still there. It seemed to him that someone from within the family circle would be the best guarantee for a harmonious marriage bond. They would have the same background and mutual understanding.

Though he was living in Canaan, Isaac was not allowed to marry a local woman because the Canaanites were under the curse of God.[4] They were heathen, for they did not worship the God of Isaac, and marrying an unbeliever would create an unequal pair in God's sight.[5]

Compare Genesis 24:3 with 2 Corinthians 6:14. What are the dangers of a marriage in which the spouses are unequally yoked?

Abraham, who desired a wife of God's choice for his son, was convinced that marriages should be made in heaven. He believed that God was personally interested in the joining together of two people. After all, hadn't He created a special wife for Adam, someone with whom the first man could enjoy an optimum of happiness?[6]

[3] Genesis 15:2-3
[4] Genesis 9:22-27
[5] 2 Corinthians 6:14
[6] Genesis 2:18

---

*Do you believe that God is personally interested
in the specific details of whom you marry?
If you are single, how should this cause you to
approach marriage? If you are married, how
should this impact how you relate to your spouse?*

Abraham believed that God had also selected a wife for
Isaac. As a father he could give his son riches, but only the
Lord could give him an understanding wife[7]—a good wife is
a gift and blessing from the Lord.[8]

Abraham was certain that God Himself would be in charge
of the trip if he asked Him.[9] Therefore, he encouraged his
steward with the promise that the Lord God would send His
angel[10] before him to ensure contact with the proper woman.

After a 550-mile journey Eliezer arrived in Harran where
Nahor, Abraham's brother, lived. He did two things upon
arrival. He prayed for help, and then, being practical, he
went to the most common gathering place in town, the well.
It was nearing evening. Soon the women would come to
fetch water.

How would he select the right wife for Isaac from the many
who would come to the well? Which one had God destined
to be the wife of the son of his master? Everything depended
upon God's leading, so Eliezer proceeded prayerfully.

[7] Proverbs 19:14
[8] Proverbs 18:22
[9] Proverbs 3:5-6
[10] Genesis 24:7

He prayed for a sign of recognition: "May the girl whom I ask for water and who offers to water my camels also be the wife You desire for Isaac." And knowing that a person can ask God for anything, he asked for success that very day.

Despite its brevity, this prayer revealed the steward's keen insight. Eastern women were very shy when meeting strange men. Therefore, if a girl responded so frankly to him, he could take this as God's leading.

But was he aware that the answer to his prayer would also reveal certain other qualities about the girl? It was no small thing to draw water for ten camels. Thirty to sixty gallons needed to be drawn and carried. That required good health and physical strength. The woman who was to be next in the chain of many offspring that God had promised to Abraham would need to be strong and healthy.

The action would also reveal something about her character. Friendliness and a willingness to serve should be characteristic of Isaac's bride. Efficiency and the ability to do hard work would be beneficial in the nomadic existence she would lead with her husband. It would also be in her favor if she showed initiative when she had ideas of her own.

———————

If you are married, what sort of characteristics did you look for in a spouse? How have those characteristics impacted your marriage?

———————

If you are single, have you thought about what sort of characteristics you look for in a spouse? How might you go about discerning those in someone?

Isaac, the son of aged parents, had remained a bachelor until after he was forty. He was strongly attached to his mother. He was not a man of great deeds. His wife would need to complement him, having qualities he didn't possess.

Abraham's servant had prayed softly to himself. No one had heard his request but God. He was scarcely finished praying when something inside him warned him to look up. There in front of him he saw a girl with a pitcher on her shoulder. Slender. Youthful. As she approached, he more strongly sensed that she was the answer to his prayer. Here was Isaac's bride!

• • •

The day had started like any other for Rebekah. There had been no indication that this would be a history-making day. She had no idea she was about to begin the leading role in a love story that would touch hearts for thousands of years to come. The daily walk to the well was prosaic, like yesterday's and like the day before yesterday's—but this day, when she arrived at the well, she sensed tension in the stranger who watched her approach. It didn't annoy her. She gladly answered his request for water.

Why is my heartbeat so light, so happy—as if it were expecting something? she wondered. It seemed as if something outside her was giving wings to her feet and extra strength to her arms. She wanted to do something especially friendly for this kindly old man. So she volunteered to draw water for his camels, too. It was a long time before the thirst of all the animals was quenched, yet the light, happy feeling stayed with her. She completed the hard work efficiently.

The searching eyes of the foreigner hadn't left her for an instant. Silently, he scrutinized her.

When the work was completed, he gave her gifts of gold. It surprised her that he would give such a rich gift for the small favor, but she could see, from the people who were with him, that he was a rich man.

"Tell me whose daughter you are."

She noticed the suppressed tension in his voice. When she answered, "I am the daughter of Bethuel. He is the son of Milkah and Nahor," he bowed his head to God and praised Him.

When she heard him mention the well-known name of her great-uncle Abraham in his prayer and realized that this godly man had made his long journey especially to meet her family, she ran home to tell them.

Because of all the excitement, no one slept very well in Bethuel's home that night. They had all come to one conclusion after hearing the man's story—this was the leading of God. They had heard how the search for Isaac's wife was anchored in the promises of the Lord. As Isaac's birth and life were proof of the fulfillment of the promises of God,[11] so was his marriage to be connected with God's promises. His trust in these promises was the reason for Abraham's actions. In sending Eliezer on the search for the bride, Abraham was convinced he was doing God's will and was sure of an answer to his prayers.[12]

What is one thing you've done in the last week that displayed active trust in God? How can you more intentionally portray to the world around you that you trust Him?

Abraham and Eliezer weren't disappointed. God had clearly shown the way.[13] God's leading was further revealed by the agreement of the relatives. In Rebekah's culture marriage was not something to be decided on only by the partners. Others, especially the parents, were involved in counseling.

Though the family had voiced its opinion, the final word was with Rebekah. She gave an unconditional yes to the question, "Will you go with this man?" Her answer was a great step in faith. The distance between her future home and her parents' city meant she probably would never return. It would be a lifetime separation. Rebekah, the granddaughter

---

[11] Romans 4:18-21; Hebrews 11:17-19
[12] 1 John 5:14-15
[13] Psalm 143:8; 32:8

of Nahor, exhibited some of the same quality of faith as Nahor's brother Abraham. When she knew God's will, she obeyed unconditionally, just as Abraham had.

She and Isaac met for the first time in a field. The closeness of the tent had been too much for Isaac. Realizing that the caravan might return any day, he had gone out to talk with God.

Prayer is a key component of active trust.
What does your prayer life look like?
What is one thing you can do this
week to grow in your prayer life?

Rebekah saw a man coming toward the caravan. When she learned that he was Isaac, she covered her face with a veil, for a bride in the East never showed her face to the groom until after the wedding ceremony.

Isaac's bride must have reminded him of his mother. Like Sarah, Rebekah was intelligent, energetic, strong-willed, and very lovely. She was everything he could desire in a woman. He loved her, and she loved him.

History is much more interesting than fairy tales because the people are made of flesh and blood, of emotions and reason, of hope and despair. Rebekah, a young, unknown girl, became a participant in the history of Abraham—the father of the Jewish faith, the father of all believers, the friend of

God. She entered on the threshold of a future full of promise. What would she make of it?

Rebekah Takes Her Lot into Her Own Hands

READ

Genesis 27:1-30, 41-46

• • •

Rebekah became suspicious when she saw her elder son, Esau, go into Isaac's tent. *What are those two talking about?* she wondered. Driven by curiosity, she spied on the man whom many years ago she had considered to be a gift from God. Unthinkable!

Communication between Rebekah and Isaac had become poor. Their family unit had crumbled. It was parted into two smaller worlds. One consisted of Jacob and herself, the other of Isaac and Esau. The boys, though twins, were as different as night and day.

Hairy Esau was a rough man, both physically and in inward character. He liked to live outdoors and had won his father's admiration because Isaac liked the meat Esau brought home from the hunt.

Jacob, the younger, was slight of build and cunning in character. He stayed at home and was his mother's favorite.

Having children should have drawn Isaac and Rebekah together, but unfortunately, it seems to have driven them apart. Their marriage was marred by partiality.

Does disunity mar any part of your family?
If so, what is something you can do this
week to move toward reconciliation?

Rebekah's love for Jacob was based on what God had said before the children were born. But on this day she had no time for contemplation. It was not a day to muse about the past. There were other things to consider. The future of her darling son, Jacob, was at stake.

Evidently it did not dawn on her that the future also concerned God's people, that it involved her husband and Esau. She neglected to consult God in her plan even though He had given distinct predictions about the future.

Rebekah, though eighty years old, had not lost her sharpness of intellect or quickness of action. She eavesdropped at her husband's door.

Isaac was over a hundred years old and was preparing for death. The blessing that God had passed on to him through Abraham,[14] he now wanted to pass on—against the Word of God—to his older son. Such a solemn act between a father and his son was always celebrated with a meal.

Rebekah was alarmed. Something was going wrong. Hadn't God clearly predicted before the children were born that the elder would serve the younger?[15] This promise of

[14] Genesis 17:1-8, 21
[15] Romans 9:10-12

God would be thwarted by what Isaac planned to do. This could not be allowed to happen.

Rebekah understood why God preferred Jacob. Esau had proven that he didn't take God's commandments seriously. He had sold the right that was his as the firstborn[16] and that is holy in the sight of God.[17] Taking it very lightly, he had exchanged it for a plate of food.[18] He had also married heathen women. All of this had caused much sorrow to his parents. And, although Jacob hadn't done the right thing when he had cunningly obtained the birthright, he had at least shown that he believed in it. His life was more God centered than Esau's.

In the past, sorrow regarding their children had caused the parents to pray. Hadn't Rebekah's pregnancy been a result of Isaac's intercession? And hadn't Rebekah sought God when she realized to her surprise that the two children were fighting with each other even during her pregnancy?[19]

If you are married, do you have unity in prayer with your spouse? How can you build more intentional prayer together into your relationship?

If you are single, who in your life can serve as your prayer companion? How might you build unity of faith into your friendship through prayer?

[16] Deuteronomy 21:15-17
[17] Exodus 13:2; Hebrews 12:16
[18] Genesis 25:29-34
[19] Genesis 25:21-23

It is interesting to note that in both cases of praying only one parent is mentioned. Is this because of the brevity of the Scripture story? Or were they already getting into the habit of not sharing their thoughts with each other? Had the spry, intelligent Rebekah ever really loved the weak Isaac, who was much older? Had Isaac ever taken the trouble to win her love? Was their intense love for their sons an escape to replace the disunity of their own hearts? Or were they driven apart because they had attributed different values to the Word of God?

What barriers keep you from truly loving someone God has placed in your path? What is one thing you can do this week to show selfless love to that person?

A marriage, which God compares with the bond between Christ and His Church, can only be happy if the partners function together. Although man and wife are equal before God,[20] they each have different responsibilities within the marriage bond. The man is the head.[21] He is responsible for his wife. He is to love her and to lead her according to the Word of God.[22] He is to honor her because she is the weaker of the two.[23] The wife must adapt herself to the husband. She is to follow his leadership.

[20] 1 Corinthians 11:11-12
[21] 1 Corinthians 11:3,9
[22] Ephesians 5:21-33
[23] 1 Peter 3:7

The secret of this relationship is Christ. The marriage is what God wants it to be when both partners subject themselves to each other because they honor Christ. Within this framework the partners fit into God's order of creation and experience the greatest possible personal fulfillment.

A woman who has this perspective wants to further the well-being of her husband: "She brings him good, not harm, all the days of her life."[24] If she manages her family guided by this conviction, her husband and children will bless her and will consider themselves fortunate.[25]

When you study Rebekah as a wife in light of Ephesians 5:21-33 and Proverbs 31:12, what conclusions can you draw?

Although Rebekah didn't have these requirements on a printed page, she must have known them, as Sarah did.[26] But she didn't act on them. Isaac was not without blame either. Had he, as her husband, not served her through leading in the way God expected?

Rebekah took her lot in her own hands. This woman who once had sufficient faith to trust God for an unknown future now felt that she had to help Him out a bit. She lacked confidence that the eternal God was mighty enough to fulfill His promises to Jacob without human intervention. She did not

[24] Proverbs 31:12
[25] Proverbs 31:28
[26] 1 Peter 3:6

take this opportunity to discuss the matter with her husband. An opportunity to grow closer together out of necessity was bypassed. She decided, without hesitation, to deceive her husband and cheat Esau.

Reflect on a time when you took a situation into your own hands, cutting out the advice and perspective of those God has placed in your life. What was the result? What did you learn from this situation?

Jacob was not concerned about the act of the deception itself, either. His only concern was that he might be discovered and bring a curse upon himself. Rebekah was prepared to do anything to further her cause. Had the gap between her and God so widened that she didn't fear His curse? She sounded reckless when she said, "My son, let the curse fall on me."[27]

The situation developed quickly. Before Esau entered his father's tent with his steaming meat dish, Jacob stole his blessing. Rebekah thought she had won, but she was wrong. She had lost. Her cunning action brought great sorrow upon Isaac. His name meant "laughing one," but he didn't have much to laugh about anymore. And if Esau had once respected his mother, he would no longer.

[27] Genesis 27:13

---

*What reasons could Rebekah have had
for taking the future of Esau and Jacob in
her own hands? See Romans 9:10-12.*

Rebekah had also harmed Jacob, her favorite. With her help he had deceived his father by lying. He had slandered God's name when he told his father that God had given him his quick success in hunting. But that was not all. Jacob had developed into a master deceiver. He could be as cunning as his mother.[28] That God blessed him despite all this was grace,[29] for Jacob certainly hadn't earned the blessing.

---

*What generational sinful tendencies exist in
your family heritage? What has God taught
you through the impact of your family?*

Jacob would later learn painfully that a deceiver will be deceived. First he would be deceived by his father-in-law,[30] then by his own children.[31] Also, how often would Jacob ask himself if he was really a man blessed by God, since his mother hadn't allowed God the chance to prove this? The stolen blessing was a doubtful possession.

It was also because of Rebekah's actions that Esau desired

[28] Genesis 30:37-43
[29] Genesis 31:11-13
[30] Genesis 29:25
[31] Genesis 37:31-35

to kill Jacob later. This again led to deception. Jacob had to flee his parents' home. Rebekah's brother, Laban, supplied a good hiding place in Harran.

After she had arranged everything with Jacob, now a man over forty years old, Rebekah went to Isaac. She said to her husband, "These foreign women are a burden. I would rather die than have Jacob marry one of them." What she said was true. Isaac and she had experienced much sorrow because of Esau's marriages. Yet she uttered no word of repentance for all she had done.

Rebekah had overestimated herself and made a false promise to Jacob that she would call for him when Esau's anger had turned away. She was unable to keep this promise because she did not live until Jacob's return. She saw her beloved son for the last time when he left to find a wife.[32] When he returned home about twenty years later,[33] his father was still alive and Esau was reconciled with him, but Rebekah was dead.

Rebekah, like Sarah, was unable to foresee the far-reaching effects of her deeds. The hatred kindled in Esau's heart continued to future generations.[34] For many centuries the Edomites, Esau's descendants, would be the enemies of Israel. Herod the Great, the man who murdered the children in Bethlehem,[35] and his son Herod Antipas, the man who ridiculed Jesus at His trial,[36] were both Edomites, men from Idumea.

[32] Genesis 28:1-4
[33] Genesis 31:41
[34] Ezekiel 25:12-13
[35] Matthew 2:16
[36] Luke 23:11

Rebekah, the woman who had been so carefully selected to be Isaac's wife, a woman chosen by God, had not fulfilled the promise expected of her. Her beginning was good, but her end was disappointing because she couldn't wait upon God.[37] She took her lot in her own hands and didn't allow God to fight for her.[38] She forgot that those who believe do not need to make haste.[39] She neglected to give God a chance to show what He can and will do for those who wait upon Him.[40]

---

[37] Psalm 27:14; 37:34
[38] Deuteronomy 1:30; Exodus 14:13
[39] Isaiah 28:16
[40] Isaiah 64:4

4

LEAH

A Woman Whose Unhappy Marriage Became God's Blessing to Humanity

This polygamous family, with many shameful things to
its discredit, was accepted by God, as a whole, to be the
beginning of the Twelve Tribes that became the Messianic
Nation, chosen by God to bring the Savior into the world.
This shows that God uses human beings as they are.

HENRY H. HALLEY, *HALLEY'S BIBLE HANDBOOK*

READ

Genesis 29:1-35

. . .

LEAH'S ILLUSIONS HAD FALLEN TO PIECES, totally broken. The
few hours of darkness that now lay behind her had been the
happiest of her life. Hoping against hope, she had lain quietly, savoring what she knew might be short-lived happiness.
While she surrendered herself to the love of her bridegroom,
at the same time she dreaded the hour of truth. She feared
the break of day.

The hour came slowly; the first sunbeam striped the
earthen tent floor. Then her bridegroom woke up and saw her,
his bride. The disappointment she had anticipated—she had

not had enough courage to prepare him—darted across his face. Her husband, Jacob, expected to see her sister, Rachel, the woman he had loved from the very first moment he had seen her seven long years ago. For Rachel he had worked, had hoped, and had dreamed. With Rachel he had expected to pass his night after the wedding. Jacob had thought of only one woman—Rachel.

He looked sleepily at Leah and then screamed as the truth rudely awakened him. Bewildered, desperate, he leaped to his feet, wondering how such a dreadful lot could have befallen him. Slowly his confusion turned to fury as he realized that he had been deceived. Under cover of the night and the bride's veil, the wrong girl had been brought to his tent because of financial and social implications.

Leah no doubt understood Jacob's sense of betrayal. He had been tricked like a person void of reason, a pawn of another's authority. A woman whom he did not love had been forced on him. As these and other thoughts cut through his being, Jacob's reaction made it utterly clear that there was no place for Leah in his heart. She meant nothing to him, even though she cared for him deeply.

There is no turning back, Leah thought to herself. *Despite everything, I am his wife. My future has been decided. I am married to a man who doesn't care about me in the least.* While she reasoned to herself, Jacob stormed out of the tent. He was surely looking for Laban, his father-in-law, who had treated him so poorly.

Leah remained in the tent alone, continuing the dialogue

of her thoughts. The future looked gloomy. But hope still existed because she loved Jacob. She simply would not and could not believe that her cause was lost. *Perhaps*, she reasoned, *the future will reveal itself to be brighter than it looks right now. Maybe Jacob will change his mind after he sees how much I love him. Maybe everything will turn out all right when I give him a son. Maybe, maybe . . .*

• • •

Jacob faced Laban, restrained fury and accusation in his voice. "What is this you have done to me?" he raged. "I served you for Rachel, didn't I? Why have you deceived me?"[1]

Laban turned slowly, looking down at his feet. His defense was weak, his excuse poor. "It is not our custom here to give the younger daughter in marriage before the older one," he answered,[2] ignoring the fact that this was an objection he should have raised earlier. The plain fact was that he had calculated the advantages he would have in such a dishonest venture. Through deceit, he had ensnared his hard-working son-in-law and now would have cheap labor even longer. This way, the groom had to pay a high bridal price. At the same time, Laban had also given his eldest daughter in marriage. She was not as pretty as Rachel and probably had been passed over by prospective suitors.

Jacob had little choice. The only thing he could do was to agree with Laban's proposal to marry Rachel also, as soon as

[1] Genesis 29:25
[2] Genesis 29:26

the seven-day wedding feast was over. That decision obliged him to serve his father-in-law for another seven years.

But Jacob also allowed his thoughts to wander back to his parental home. Long ago he had cheated his father in a similar way by impersonating his brother. He, the youngest son, had stolen the blessing that belonged to his brother, Esau.[3] The deceiver had been deceived, defeated with his own weapon. He now suffered the same sorrow he had inflicted upon others.

Thus Leah began her first days of married life, the only days that she had her husband to herself. The man who in his thoughts was already with another woman could not wait to call that woman his own. Leah craved a love that she did not receive. Would she ever receive it?

Have you ever felt a lack of love from someone in your life? How did you respond? What did God teach you through that experience?

Her marriage showed little resemblance to the covenant between the partners God had in mind when He created man and woman for one another. God's plan for marriage was monogamy, the coming together of one man with one woman.[4]

The Israelites, however, disobeyed God and began to take

[3] Genesis 27:5-40
[4] Genesis 1:27; 2:24

other wives like the heathens around them. Although God tolerated this, He also knew that no man could violate His order of creation without paying for it. That pain is what Leah experienced. She tasted the bitter fruit of polygamy— wedlock of one man with more than one woman—every day of her life.

As the years passed since that first wedding night, the door to her husband's heart remained tightly closed for Leah. Part of this was due to her looks; she couldn't compare in physical beauty with her sister. Her eyes, for example, were tender and weak, though the exact nature of the problem is unknown. Did she, like so many in her country, suffer from an eye disease that made her looks offensive? Was she cross-eyed? Were her eyes healthy but lacking the color and sparkle that made other Eastern beauties so attractive? Were they a pale blue instead of a shining brown?

Although handicapped in this one important area of her life, Leah nevertheless was blessed by God in a special way. "When the LORD saw that Leah was not loved," the Bible reads, "he enabled her to conceive."[5] God was not hindered by the fact that Leah was not attractive. He did not judge her by her outward appearance. He looked at her heart, which was reaching out toward Him.[6] Rachel's heart, on the other hand, was rapidly becoming selfish and self-centered.

Sorrow often brings with it a hidden danger. It can make

---

[5] Genesis 29:31
[6] 1 Samuel 16:7

a person self-centered, shutting him or her off from other people, the outside world, and God. In Leah's life, though, the opposite was true. Her sorrow drove her to God. This is seen in the names of her sons.

She named her firstborn Reuben, which meant, "He has seen my affliction." Her thought behind this name was that God had noticed her trouble. She knew that anyone could trust God with great confidence. Hadn't God promised that if someone called on Him, He would answer and also show that person His salvation?[7] Leah, who had experienced God's faithfulness and love, expressed that certainty at the birth of her second son, Simeon. "Cast your cares on the LORD and he will sustain you," the psalmist David would sing centuries later.[8] "When I am afraid, I put my trust in you."[9]

Simeon's name meant, "The Lord has heard." As often as she mentioned the name Simeon, she reminded herself and those around her of God's goodness. Leah shared her problems with God and did not forget to honor Him openly after He answered her prayers, something that He expected from His people.[10]

Has God recently answered one of your prayers? How can you honor Him openly when He answers prayer?

[7] Psalm 91:15-16
[8] Psalm 55:22
[9] Psalm 56:3
[10] Psalm 50:15

The twelve tribes of Israel—named after Jacob's sons—would refer to God's faithfulness until the end of human history. A tremendous heritage would come through Leah, the woman with the unhappy marriage. Sorrow in Leah's life was God's instrument; it caused her to become a building stone of the house of Israel. Later generations would praise her for that.[11]

The natural longing after her husband's love—it could not be otherwise—remained. But the absence of it brought Leah to a greater understanding of God. Her life was enriched by her sorrow, ripened by testing. Her confidence in God grew.

———

Consider a past experience with sorrow.
Did it drive you toward God, or away from Him?
Have you observed any ways in which your
life has been "ripened by testing"?

———

When her fourth son, Judah, was born, the love for God in Leah's heart was stronger than her love for Jacob. "This time I will praise the LORD," she exclaimed jubilantly.[12] For the first time, she did not mention the love of her husband. She was not aware of the prophetic meaning of this moment. She didn't know that with Judah's birth a new era was beginning. From the descendants of this son, out of the tribe of Judah, the Messiah would come. Every generation would praise the name of Judah.

---

[11] Ruth 4:11
[12] Genesis 29:35

The beauty of Leah's growing relationship with God is highlighted in how He honored her faithful and increasingly dependent perspective. What blessings from God have you seen emerge after you chose faithfulness in a difficult time?

Leah would never know how privileged she was. This fact would only be revealed many centuries later. Leah was used by God to be a blessing to all humanity. Indeed, through her the birth of the Savior of the world—Jesus Christ—came nearer.

Meanwhile, her life didn't proceed without tensions. Again and again Leah gave herself to a husband who didn't love her. For Leah, the joy of coming together as marriage partners had a bitter taste. With unfailing intuition, she sensed that her surrender of love did not set Jacob's heart aflame. The marriage act performed in this way was humiliating to her. It became an insult. Yet the strange fact remained that, while Jacob loved Rachel, Leah gave birth to his children.

Contrary to other women of the Bible,[13] Leah did not become proud when Rachel remained childless. Leah was open and humble despite her sister's envy. Yet the atmosphere in the family remained heavy and explosive. Little incidents revealed how touchy the situation was. One day, for example, Reuben wanted to surprise his mother with

---

[13] Genesis 16:4-5; 1 Samuel 1:2-7

mandrakes—small prune-like fruits also called "love apples." Some people of that day believed that the mandrakes caused riches, happiness, and even fertility. Envious of the attention Leah received from her son, Rachel wanted some mandrakes. "Give me some of your son's mandrakes," she demanded.[14]

Her demands led to a strong argument in which Leah also lost her composure. "Wasn't it enough that you took away my husband?" she replied sharply. "Will you take my son's mandrakes too?"[15]

Rachel knew how to get what she wanted. "Jacob will sleep with you tonight because of the mandrakes," she promised.[16] Rachel, the younger of the two sisters and the second wife, extended her favors to Leah in a superior way.

It was an unworthy proposal in light of the holiness of wedlock and basic principles of human rights. Yet Leah accepted the bullying by her sister. The woman who was willing to do everything she could to win her husband's love humiliated herself once again.

When Jacob returned home from work that evening, Leah was waiting for him. Like a dog begging for the favor of his master, Leah hankered after Jacob's affection. "You must sleep with me," she begged. "I have hired you."[17] It was a miracle that the holy God still accepted people who made such a mockery of things He considered holy. Marriage and love had to be treated with respect.

[14] Genesis 30:14
[15] Genesis 30:15
[16] Genesis 30:15, author's paraphrase
[17] Genesis 30:16

What are some specific ways you can treat marriage (your own and/or the marriages of those around you) with respect? How can you encourage and support the marriages in your community?

Leah rapidly gave birth to two more sons, Issachar and Zebulun. Both names again resounded the love of God.

Leah also became the only one of Jacob's wives to give him a daughter, Dinah.

By this time, Jacob was married not only to Leah and Rachel but to the two maids as well. The struggle to become the best had brought Rachel to offer her servant girl to her husband. Leah, who did not want to be left behind, did the same. Those two women—Bilhah and Zilpah—increased the family with two sons each.

Despite the unworthy manner with which this marriage was treated, the quick expansion of the family fit into God's plan. The promise He had given to Jacob's grandfather, Abraham—that he would become a great nation—had to be fulfilled.[18] It was also God's promise to Jacob.[19]

Leah, with her deep-seated faith, had a prominent place in that plan. She brought six of the twelve sons—heads of tribes—into the world. But her life didn't become any easier. She never won Jacob's love. As long as Leah lived, Jacob always preferred Rachel.

[18] Genesis 12:2
[19] Genesis 28:14-15

Leah experienced this partiality again when the family returned to the Promised Land. As they neared the border, Jacob became afraid of his brother, Esau, whom he had tricked twenty years before and from whose wrath he had fled the county.[20] Scared of what his vengeful brother might do to his entire family, he divided it into small groups. First came his concubines and their sons. Then Leah and her children followed the first group. The most protected places in the rear were reserved for Joseph and Rachel. Rachel was farthest from the threatening danger.

Leah, the woman with the weak eyes, is recorded in history as the woman with the unhappy marriage. The Bible does not say whether Jacob refused her only because of her appearance. Maybe her disposition and character differed so much from those of her husband that harmonious unity was never formed. One thing is certain, however. Leah wept many bitter tears during her lifetime.

Shortly before his death, Jacob met with Joseph and during that meeting described how he had buried Rachel near Ephrath in Canaan.[21] Then Jacob called his sons together to foretell their futures and told them that Leah had been buried in the family's burial cave at Machpelah. Thus Leah, after her death, was placed with honor alongside Abraham, Sarah, Isaac, and Rebekah.[22]

Leah's story is both a warning and an encouragement. Her life stands as a warning for people not to make decisions against the will of God. She also brings to a standstill those

---

[20] Genesis 27
[21] Genesis 48:7
[22] Genesis 49:30-31

people who try to treat love lightly or who expect to win the love of a life partner after the wedding vows have been exchanged.

But the story of Leah also serves as an encouragement because it gives us further insight into how God looks at a person. He based His evaluation of Leah on her heart and not on her appearance. He also accepted her in the situation as it appeared to Him. Through His love, He can and will transform a person with a nearly unbearable life burden into a channel through whom His blessings for humanity can flow.

5

DINAH

A Girl Whose Curiosity Turned into Mourning

Turning a human being into a thing, an object, is almost always the first step toward justifying violence against that person.

JEAN KILBOURNE, "TWO WAYS A WOMAN CAN GET HURT"

READ

Genesis 34:1-15, 24-29

• • •

DINAH, THE DAUGHTER OF JACOB, FELT BORED—and she had good reason to be. Life in a goatskin tent did not offer much attraction for a girl in her teens, especially since her parents were aged and she had only brothers with whom to talk. Dinah had not had much of a chance to relax. Her life had been nomadic, constantly on the move. Originally migrating from the city of Harran in Mesopotamia[1]—about four hundred miles to the northeast—her family continued to wander. Again and again after her family halted for a while,

---

[1] Genesis 31:18

the tent pins would be taken out of the ground and on they would go. They would be on the move once more, moving step by step to keep pace with the animals.

Have you ever felt displaced? All of us occasionally feel lonely or uprooted. What was your petition to God during that time? In what ways did He answer?

Then they arrived in Canaan. Dinah's father pitched their tents near Shalem, which belonged to the city of Shechem, and bought a piece of land.[2] Apparently he wanted to settle in the land God had promised to his forefathers Abraham and Isaac, for through the promise the land was also his.

It was remarkable, however, that Jacob did not travel several more miles to Bethel. There he had made a promise to God some twenty years earlier, shortly before he moved out of Canaan.[3] Had his love for God cooled off?

Shechem was situated in the strategic pass that cut through the Ebal, Ephraim, and Gerizim Mountains, and it controlled the roads to the north and the west. Boasting a beautiful location and advanced culture, Shechem was never dull. Daily, the merchants and migrants who traveled from the East to Egypt passed through the city in exotic dress.

Dinah was bored of being alone. She was restless. She

[2] Genesis 33:18-20
[3] Genesis 28:19-22; 31:13

longed for something happier, brighter than the tents of her father. She wanted to meet other girls and had heard that the girls of Shechem offered a colorful picture because of their beautiful Eastern clothes. Desiring to see these costumes for herself, she left the parental tent and began walking toward Shechem.

Have you ever made an imprudent decision out of boredom or restlessness? What was the result?

Why did no one prevent Dinah from leaving? Why did no one warn her? Hadn't her mother or father pointed out the possible dangers threatening her? In the past, Great-grandmother Sarah and Grandmother Rebekah had found themselves in great trouble when they had drawn much attention from the kings of the lands they visited.[4] Only an intervention by God and the presence of their husbands had kept them from disaster. But Dinah was alone, young, and inexperienced. In this culture, daughters were under the strict supervision of their parents. Her father should have been a protection over her life, but he was absent from her story until after she wandered into danger. Was his lack of engagement and wisdom in guiding his daughter a possible sign of his cooled relationship with God?

[4] Genesis 12:14-20; 26:7-11

What protection has God built in the community around you? Who in your life provides the wisdom to hem you in from disaster?

So she arrived at Shechem. How many, if any, of the local beauties she saw is unknown. But she did end up in the bedroom of the prince of the land. Prince Shechem, the son of Hamor, saw her, took her, and raped her.

Her little trip, launched in curiosity and impulse, set off a chain reaction of misery that ended with crime and mourning. The comfortable relationship that Jacob and his family had with the heathen land unleashed a sorrow so great that it could not be reversed after it was set in motion.

Rape is a horrible crime that no woman deserves, no matter the situation. Jacob's disengagement from his daughter, and his failure to prevent his family from drawing so close to the heathen city, laid the groundwork for Dinah to stumble into a dangerous place. Scripture calls blessed the person who "does not walk in the counsel of the wicked, nor stand in the path of sinners, nor sit in the seat of scoffers" (Psalm 1:1, NASB). There is wisdom in avoiding situations abounding with sin. In what areas of your life might you be drawing too close to the "path of sinners"?

While Dinah remained in the royal palace with Shechem, Jacob and his sons heard what had happened. King Hamor, Shechem's father, anticipated Jacob's response and visited him. "My son has his heart set on your daughter," he said. "Please give her to him as his wife."[5]

Then Shechem himself arrived. He had horribly violated Dinah, and perhaps he and his father had come to the conclusion that she should become his wife to keep peace with Jacob and his family. Regardless, he asked Jacob to give Dinah to him to legitimize his actions. "Let me find favor in your eyes, and I will give you whatever you ask," he told Jacob. "Make the price for the bride and the gift I am to bring as great as you like, and I'll pay whatever you ask me. Only give me the young woman as my wife."[6] It was clear that Shechem felt very attached to Dinah. He loved her and talked tenderly to her. And she? Scripture does not give her a voice. Was she terrified? Had she, knowing that the violation meant no other man would marry her, pushed away thoughts of the rape and clung to hope for a marriage to Shechem?

In order to please Dinah's family as much as possible, Hamor suggested that Jacob and his tribe make a covenant with the people of Shechem so that they could intermarry and do business together. But Simeon and Levi, Dinah's brothers, were furious. Under their existing law, the loss of a girl's virginity was considered a flagrant crime.[7] They were too shocked and angry to overlook the insult, for it was an outrage against all of them. "You can't do such a thing!" they raged.

---

[5] Genesis 34:8
[6] Genesis 34:11-12
[7] Deuteronomy 22:20-21

Their fury was justified, but the way they took their revenge was not. Just as Jacob's lack of relational closeness to God had left Dinah open to being preyed upon, his lack of guiding wisdom in the lives of his sons meant they turned to sinful reasoning and action rather than the ways of God. Rather than acting honestly, Simeon and Levi moved hypocritically. Pretending to agree with King Hamor's proposal to merge the two groups of people, they set forth the condition that every male inhabitant of Shechem would have to undergo circumcision, the ritual that was obligatory for the Hebrew men. Their request revealed how superficially the two brothers thought about religion. They mistook its true meaning for its outward sign. And, what was far worse, they used religion to cover up premeditated murder.

*Have you ever used religion as
an excuse or cover for personal
decisions? How did that impact your
relationship with God? With others?*

After Hamor and Shechem convinced their subjects of the reasonableness of the Hebrews' request, the ceremony took place. Simeon and Levi then entered the city on the third day armed with swords. While the entire male population was in pain, unable to move because of their wounds, Simeon and Levi killed every man in the city. With their swords, they beheaded or stabbed man after man. They didn't hesitate even to slaughter Hamor and Shechem, men with whom they had pretended to discuss the covenant only a few days before. What began with lack of relationship with God ended up becoming murder.

Simeon and Levi's gruesome murder of unsuspecting people wasn't even enough to cool their hatred. They also plundered the city, seizing all the flocks and herds and capturing the women and children as their prey.

The sons of Jacob had met one heinous crime with another. Simeon and Levi had become murderers, abhorred by the world. They had cast a blame upon themselves that could never be removed. Countless men died because of their cruelty; wives and children became widows and homeless orphans who could call sorrow their only personal possession.

"You have made me stink among all the people of this land," Jacob lamented to Simeon and Levi. "We are so few that they will come and crush us, and we will all be killed."[8]

It was in fact God's name—so closely connected with Jacob's name and the names of His people[9]—that really suffered. Jacob neglected to mention this. Was it possible that he was more concerned with his own name, the talk that went on behind his back, than with the honor of God? Again we see signs that the weakness and distance from God on the part of the father led to the misfortune of his daughter and the sin of his sons.

---

[8] Genesis 34:30, author's paraphrase
[9] Genesis 32:28-29

Are you more concerned about your name and reputation—or God's? How do you exhibit this in your life and attitude?

Jacob's attitude toward his family was not impressive either. He rebuked Simeon and Levi for the way they had brought disgrace to him, but he did not mention their sin against God and their fellow humans.

The Bible doesn't even mention Jacob's fatherly concern and authority concerning Dinah. She didn't receive the attention from him that she needed before, during, or after this painful situation. Jacob was thinking only about himself.

Whether or not Dinah's mother understood and comforted her is not recorded. Yet who else but Leah—who had suffered so much herself—could have been more understanding of her daughter's pain? The scars from Dinah's emotional wounds may never have healed completely.

After these sad events, on God's command Jacob moved his family away from the site of the crime to Bethel. There Jacob once again became the man he ought to have been earlier, a father who led his family in the service of God. But Dinah's story remains a tragic reminder that distance from God can lead to tragedy not only in our own lives but in the lives of those we love.

6
TAMAR

A Neglected Woman Who Vindicated Her Rights

We males would all be better off if God-gifted women were vigorously exercising their talents on our behalf and calling us to account where we have acted selfishly or unjustly towards them or others.

JOHN SCANZONI, "ASSERTIVENESS FOR CHRISTIAN WOMEN"

READ

Genesis 38:6-30

• • •

TAMAR, WHOSE NAME MEANT "PALM TREE," adjusted her long dress. Held together with a girdle tied around her waist, the folds flowed around her slim figure and nearly touched the ground. She glanced pensively at the widow's dress she had just taken off, and then remembered that her veil had to be put on just right.

Again Tamar looked at herself. Years ago she had often worn colorful clothing, but now she hardly remembered the joy of those occasions. Although she looked younger in this outfit, there was no joy in her glance. Her eyes were serious, and around her mouth were lines of unspoken grief. She was a lonely and neglected widow.

Her movements were resolute; she knew what she wanted. She had weighed the consequences of the decision that had slowly ripened within her and knew the costs could be high. With a heavy heart, she was about to carry out a plan that she had hoped to avoid entirely.

The time had come for her to seek her rights, out of necessity, because no one else was looking after her interests. For years she had been waiting for a word from her father-in-law, Judah, but the word never came. *Judah*, she mused, *would rather forget me entirely*. Therefore, she was on her way to meet him.

As Tamar closed the door of her parental home where she had been living, she relived some of the experiences she once had with Judah and his sons.

How proud she had been when Judah had chosen her to be the bride of Er, his eldest son. Judah was the son of Jacob, the honored elder who had come to live in Canaan from the far country of Mesopotamia. Next to his riches and many sons, Jacob was known for his worship of the God of heaven and earth. He and his family did not serve sun or moon gods, nor idols of wood and stone. The eternal God was their Lord, and that made them special.

Naturally, these factors had raised Tamar's expectations. She had considered herself privileged to marry Er. But everything had gone differently from how she had hoped. Her new husband did not prove to be a godly man at all. In fact, his deeds so aroused God's anger that He took Er's life.

The laws of the tribe to which Tamar now belonged prohibited a childless woman from remaining a widow. The leaders believed that the name of a man could not, under any circumstances, go into oblivion.

Being a daughter-in-law, Tamar remained under the authority of her father-in-law after the death of her husband. It was his job to arrange Tamar's second marriage. "Marry your sister-in-law, Tamar," he said to his second son, Onan. "Our law requires this of a dead man's brother; so that her sons from you will be your brother's heirs."[1]

Onan fulfilled his duty and married her, but in appearance only. Their marriage was in fact only a sham. By purposely preventing his new wife's pregnancy, Onan refused to keep the memory of his brother alive and to bring new heirs into the world.

This caused Tamar great sorrow. Onan not only insulted her, but also injured God's institution of holy matrimony. He intentionally sabotaged the continuation of Judah's offspring. He did this not once but over and over again.

God could not forgive this sin, especially since the promised Messiah would come out of the tribe of Judah. This prediction would be clearly foretold later, at the death of Jacob.[2] How much Judah and his sons were already aware of this fact is not known. But the unknown future did not make Onan's attitude any less despicable.

[1] Genesis 38:8, author's paraphrase
[2] Genesis 49:8-10

Are you avoiding obeying something
God has asked of you? If so, why?

After Onan, like his brother Er, had been put to death by God for his sins, Tamar became a widow for the second time. Her trust in religion and in men in general had been badly damaged. The only person she still seemed to trust was Judah, her father-in-law.

"Wait to marry again until my youngest son, Shelah, has grown up," Judah had said. "Then he will become your husband."[3]

So Tamar returned to her parental home to wait until Shelah was old enough to marry her. It was the only thing a widow of that time could do. She could not live an independent life or pursue further personal development. A single woman or widow simply had to do what she was told to do.

The days became weeks, the weeks months, and the months years without producing a change in Tamar's circumstances. Gradually it dawned on Tamar that Shelah would never come for her. Judah was afraid that his youngest son would also die after marrying her, so he prevented their marriage. Tamar began to understand that people blamed her for the deaths of her two husbands. Rather than recognizing the misbehavior of his sons, Judah was placing the blame on her.

With the dawn of recognition, Tamar stopped trusting

---

[3] Genesis 38:11, author's paraphrase

Judah. Blocked out of the whole affair of her marriage, she had never been asked for an opinion. No one had even inquired about her feelings. She was considered to be only a woman without rights, free to be treated by a man as he pleased. The curse pronounced on Eve, that the man would rule over the woman, also rested on her.[4]

---

*How does the curse pronounced on
Eve manifest itself in our world today?
How can you advocate for women who are
exploited, subjugated, and forgotten?*

But Tamar was not going to put up with such an attitude. Although hurt by the humiliating treatment she had received, she did not try to seek comfort from another husband. She respected her father-in-law's request, despite the fact that she knew that Shelah would not marry her for any price. She knew that Judah probably wanted to forget that her name had been registered in his tribe.

Understanding that all the responsibility would shift to her when she took matters into her own hands, Tamar refused to neglect her duty. The command to fill the earth had been the first responsibility given to the man and the woman equally.[5] She had been given the responsibility to produce an heir for her late husband. Just because the man was not fulfilling his God-given obligation was no excuse for

[4] Genesis 3:16
[5] Genesis 1:28

her to forsake her duties as well, she felt. As a human being, she would have to give a personal account of her action to God. Regardless of her freedom to escape that obligation, Tamar refused to compromise.

The duty to give birth to an heir weighed heavily on her. She understood intuitively that the extinction of Judah's tribe had to be prevented at all costs and considered what she was about to do a religious duty. For these reasons, Tamar prepared herself for a meeting with her father-in-law.

Meanwhile, Judah was on his way from Adullam to Timnah. He looked forward to the days ahead of him. Like his forefathers—Abraham, Isaac, and Jacob—he was a wealthy shepherd and was going to Timnah to oversee the annual shepherding events. After the extensive work of shearing the sheep had been skillfully completed, there would be a great feast. For weeks everybody had been talking about this feast, for it would have an abundance of special food and drinks.

Judah became excited as he thought about the events to come. The time just behind him had not been without cares. For years, there was great sorrow in his life because of his dead sons. Recently the loss of his wife had added one more burden to his shoulders.

But the time of mourning was now past, and Judah wanted to relax. He wanted to take his place in society once more. So he traveled in full array. His identification seal that hung around his neck on a silver and gold cord showed passersby that he was a distinguished man. In his hand was the staff, a token of dignity showing that he was the head of his tribe.

As he walked, he noticed a woman on the side of the road near the entrance to the village of Enaim. A veil covered her face and prevented any meeting from having a personal touch. *She is a prostitute*, thought Judah. The woman's veil didn't bother him, for he was not interested in interacting with the woman as a person. She only aroused his desires for an object to satisfy his sexual needs.

Sin against others often arises out of a failure to consider that they are made in the image of God, created by Him and offered salvation by Him, just as we are. Whom in your life are you not treating with the honor and dignity afforded one made in the image of God? How can you adjust your actions toward that person?

With the promised reward of a young goat in return for her sexual services, the woman agreed to the act. It was the usual payment offered for this sin, and Judah expected that it would be sacrificed in the temple of the goddess of fertility, to whom prostitutes often dedicated themselves.

The woman, however, was not prepared to take him at his word. Apparently she feared that the promised goat would fail to arrive. "Will you give me something as a pledge until you send it?" she asked.[6] Judah left the choice with her. When she requested the signs of his honor and dignity—his identification seal and his walking stick—he handed them to her without hesitation.

After they had met, Judah continued on his way toward Timnah. Tamar—for it was indeed she—returned to her parental home and exchanged her veil for her widow's clothing. Life continued as if nothing had happened, at least for a while.

When Judah, by means of a friend, delivered the goat in exchange for the seal and the staff, he was unable to find the woman. When he asked the men of Enaim during his investigation where he could find the prostitute, they were astonished. "A prostitute?" they answered. "No, we do not know her. We have never had one here!"

Judah, who had not allowed God to guide his actions in this situation, now feared what other people would say. If they found out what he had done, he would certainly become a laughingstock among his people. With great impact it dawned on him how he had been blinded by his sexual desires. He had acted thoughtlessly and had put his reputation at stake. The only thing left for him to do was to forget the situation entirely, hoping there would be no further consequences. He tried to forget that the woman, also, could suffer consequences for her moral transgression. He knew that she could lose her life for her sin. Later that punishment would be laid down in God's laws.

---

[6] Genesis 38:17

Have you ever tried to hide a
transgression in the hopes that
you won't face the consequences?
What was the result?

Three months later the storm broke over Tamar's head. By then, her father-in-law had heard that she was pregnant, clearly as a result of immorality. Judah's fury knew no bounds, and he was right. Tamar had stained the name of his tribe. She was the widow of his two eldest sons and was still considered to be the future bride of his youngest son. As the head of the family, he held the responsibility to judge the sin Tamar had committed. No one can disregard the holy institution of marriage without being punished.[7]

His judgment was ruthless, inexorable. Tamar had to suffer the strongest punishment that could be applied to her transgression. Without inquiring after the facts of her case, Judah sentenced her to death. "Bring her out and have her burned to death!" he shouted.[8]

Was this judgment tainted by a mingling of fear and anger? Did Judah take into account his own thoughts toward Tamar in connection with the death of his sons? Would the burning of Tamar also burn his feelings of self-accusation, the result of his breach of promise concerning Shelah and her?

[7] Hebrews 13:4
[8] Genesis 38:24

*Consider a time when you passed
judgment on someone in your
own heart. What personal sin
might that have arisen from?*

Calm and dignified, Tamar appeared in her widow's dress. Shortly before she arrived at the site of execution, she gave something to one of the men escorting her. "Take these things to my father-in-law," she said, handing him an identification seal and a staff. "Ask him if he recognizes them," she continued with emphasis. "Tell him that the man who owns these is the father of my child."[9]

Judah's reaction was revealing. He was appalled. His own sin was crudely exposed by his personal effects. He couldn't conceal it any longer. He had to confess with shame that Tamar had vindicated the legal rights that he had kept from her. "She is more righteous than I," he acknowledged, "since I wouldn't give her to my son Shelah."[10]

Did Judah remember that he was the one who was truly guilty? She had not seduced him; he had taken her. His deed was motivated by unlawful physical desire, while her motives had been noble. She had been thinking of the continuation of Israel's posterity. From her viewpoint, she had simply done what she had thought to be her duty.

If Judah had been more honest with himself, he would

[9] Genesis 38:25, author's paraphrase.
[10] Genesis 38:26

have had to acknowledge that he had used two measuring sticks. He had used a double standard and wanted to see Tamar killed for an offense he had also committed himself.

Study the story of Judah and
Tamar in light of Romans 2:1-2.
What is your conclusion?

Six months later, Tamar brought two sons into the world, Perez and Zerah. A marriage with Shelah was now out of the question, as well as redundant. Judah had served as his replacement. Shelah did not have to marry Tamar, for justice had been done.

Many years later, Matthew wrote down the genealogy of Jesus Christ.[11] It is a long list of names, mainly of men. Of the five women mentioned, Tamar is the first. Mary, the mother of Jesus, closes the list.

Tamar, the abused woman, is the first registered woman in the genealogy of Jesus Christ. Her son Perez became a fore-father in the lineage of Jesus of Nazareth. This fact is not proof that God approved of sin. But it does confirm the fact that He wrote history straight through the failings of men.

The Bible is not a gallery of heroes. It gives the accounts of sinful people who experienced, much to their happy surprise, that they could fit into the plan God had for this

---

[11] Matthew 1:1-17

world. God's plans found their beginning and completion, their fulfillment, in Jesus Christ.

Christ's love for human beings was also proven by the publication of this genealogy. As far as His earthly life was concerned, Christ not only was prepared to come from a family of men and women of dubious quality but also was willing to emphasize that point in order to demonstrate the depth of His love. He was not afraid to identify with every sinful person who played a part in His earthly background.

Christ also did something very special for women in general while He was on earth. He gave them back their position, their value. He gave them back the place God had originally made for them before Eve's fall in the Garden. He approached them with respect, without prejudice, and treated every woman with objectivity and love. He nailed unequal treatment between men and women to the cross. Double moral standards were foreign and offensive to Him.

One day, for example, the Jewish leaders brought a woman to Jesus who had been caught in the very act of adultery.[12] Behind their pious pretext to obey the law of Moses, which says that a woman should be killed for such an offense, they were trying to trap Jesus and condemn the woman at the same time.

Jesus did not excuse the sin the woman had committed. He did, however, expose her accusers. "All right," he said sternly. "Hurl the stones at her until she dies. But only he who has never sinned may throw the first!"[13]

[12] John 8:3-11
[13] John 8:7, author's paraphrase.

Do you see any relation between what is said of Christ in Isaiah 53:10 and of Tamar? If so, what?

The accusers of the woman did not begin to heave rocks. Instead, they moved stealthily away. The Savior had touched them in their very hearts by revealing their dishonest and unloving prejudice.

Tamar's story only gains perspective when the light of Jesus Christ shines on it. Despite everything that can be said against her, Tamar became an enviable woman. Jesus Christ extended to her the honor of becoming a mother in the early history of His earthly family.

What light does the inclusion of these women in the genealogy throw on the person of Christ?

7

NAOMI

A Widow Who Cared about the Well-Being of Others

Let no one ever come to you without coming away better and happier. Be the living expression of God's kindness: kindness in your face, kindness in your eyes, kindness in your smile, kindness in your warm greeting.

MOTHER TERESA

READ

Ruth 1:1-6, 15-22; Ruth 4:14-17

• • •

NAOMI, THE WIDOW OF ELIMELECH, looked affectionately at the newborn baby on her lap. Usually not at a loss for words, she now found none to express her gratitude. Her emotions were overflowing.

Around her buzzed the voices of excited neighbor women. "Ruth has a son," they shouted happily. "Praise the Lord, Naomi. In your old age there will be a man to take care of you. But far more important, there is a redeemer for your family. We pray," continued the women, "that this little boy will become famous in Israel."[1]

---

[1] Ruth 4:14, author's paraphrase

Naomi laughed. The name of her husband, which meant "my God is king," would continue to be passed on. His inheritance would not be given to others. The names of her dead sons would not be forgotten.

She looked again at the little baby. He had been named Obed, which meant "servant." She prayed silently that the Lord God of Israel would truly be king in Obed's life. Then she thought of Elimelech, and a flood of memories pressed themselves on her.

Reflecting back, she saw herself traveling with her husband and two sons from Judah to Moab many years earlier to escape the famine that had broken out in Israel. This famine was so widespread that even in their city of Bethlehem (called "the house of bread"), there had hardly been any food available, despite the fact that the city was considered to be the granary of the country.

Elimelech had felt the responsibility for his family heavily, especially since his sons, Mahlon and Kilion, were both sick and slowly wasting away. "Let's emigrate," Elimelech had proposed. "Let's go to Moab, where there will be food for all of us. There we won't have to worry."[2]

How differently everything turned out, Naomi thought.

Moab was the country east of the Dead Sea inhabited by the descendants of Lot, the nephew of the patriarch Abraham.[3] It was not just a neighboring country. It was a nation that God had cursed because its people had been

---

[2] Ruth 1:1, author's paraphrase
[3] Genesis 19:36-37

cruel toward the Israelites after their exodus from Egypt.[4]
A Moabite was unholy in the sight of God and as such was
not allowed to enter the assembly of the Lord.

Among these people, Elimelech, Naomi, and their sons
made their home. But after they had been there only a short
time, Elimelech died.

Since they were living in Moab, the sons took wives from
among the Moabites. Mahlon married Ruth, and Kilion
married Orpah. As the years passed, though, Naomi became
painfully aware that both marriages had remained childless.
Is God keeping His blessing from us? she asked herself. Like
every Israelite, she believed that children were a blessing
from God and that the withholding of them was a proof of
His curse.[5]

Then Kilion and Mahlon, her only children, died while
still young men. Within a period of ten years, all this sorrow
had come on her. Naturally she had been lonely. Alone—
away from her country, deprived of her family, feeling forsaken by God—she had anticipated a bleak future without
meaning or perspective.

---

*Have you ever felt alone, forsaken
by God? In hindsight, did God
reveal Himself to you through those
circumstances? If so, how?*

---

[4] Deuteronomy 23:3-4; Jeremiah 48:1-47
[5] Deuteronomy 28:4, 18

Then Naomi had heard that food was once again plentiful in Bethlehem. God was blessing His people by giving them good crops. This miracle had confirmed her suspicions. The famine in the past had indeed been God's warning to His disobedient people.[6]

She realized that her family's departure from Bethlehem had, in fact, been a journey away from God. In Bethlehem she and Elimelech had been prominent citizens. *If only we had confessed our sins before God*, she thought, *perhaps we could have led our people back to Him*. But her family had missed their chance by leaving the country.

In light of God's laws, the marriage of her sons had not been acceptable. An Israelite who married a foreigner acted against the commandments of God,[7] who had given this instruction to keep His people from wandering away from Him.

Naomi's conviction had continued to grow stronger. *I must go back*, she thought. *I can no longer stay in this foreign country. I belong in Israel, in Bethlehem.*

Although she had suffered from the deaths of her family, she had also experienced rich blessings in the persons of Orpah and Ruth. When Naomi prepared herself to return to her homeland, both young women had, without hesitation, decided to leave their parents and go with her.

Naomi had always felt a strong responsibility for those women because they were the widows of her deceased sons. But that had not been the only reason. They were also heathen

[6] Leviticus 26:14-20
[7] Deuteronomy 7:3-4

women who did not know God. She had often shared with them her faith in God, the God whom she had aggrieved but still loved intensely despite everything.

Her interest in Orpah and Ruth had also helped her forget her own sorrow. It had been good to be mindful of the well-being of others; she had become refreshed from her giving. Shortly thereafter they had left Moab.

How has relationship with others encouraged you in a difficult time? How can you be an encouragement by being in relationship with others who are going through difficulties?

On the way to Bethlehem, Naomi had suddenly become aware of the finality of her daughters-in-law's decisions. Weren't their futures totally dependent on new marriages for each of them?

Certainly the thought that her daughters-in-law might one day belong to other husbands had been painful. The always-dormant suffering from the deaths of her sons had surfaced once again. But simultaneously her thoughts about the well-being of Ruth and Orpah had overruled those feelings. Gradually, as the thoughts about her sons had moved to the background, she wanted their widows to find opportunities for new happiness.

Yet Orpah and Ruth, knowing the facts, had chosen to

go with her. Instead of returning to their homes, where they would find happiness, they sought to enter a country prejudiced against them. No law-abiding Israelite would even consider the possibility of marrying a Moabitess.

"Go back, each of you, to your mother's home," Naomi had begged. "May the LORD show you kindness, as you have shown kindness to your dead husbands and to me."[8]

Seeking the best of others is often a sacrifice. When has someone done this for you? How did it make you feel?

Orpah and Ruth, however, had totally rejected her proposal. "No," they had answered tearfully. "We want to go with you to your people."[9]

Naomi, however, had not changed her mind, not even after her own future flashed before her. Her life would be even emptier. Not only would she be without a husband and children; she would also lose her daughters-in-law. But God had given her the grace not to be selfish, and so she was willing to sacrifice her desires for a secure life in old age for the welfare of the two women.

The three widows had stood together on a lonely, sunbathed road, each unable to master her tearful emotions. Suddenly one of the standing figures moved. Orpah walked

[8] Ruth 1:8
[9] Ruth 1:10, author's paraphrase.

up to Naomi, embraced her, and then turned back toward Moab. Ruth then approached her mother-in-law and clung to her.

"Your sister-in-law is going back to her people and her gods," Naomi said. "Go back with her."[10] But Ruth vehemently shook her head.

"Don't urge me to leave you or to turn back from you. Where you go I will go, and where you stay I will stay. Your people will be my people and your God my God," Ruth said.[11]

"Your God will be my God." These words had deeply touched Naomi. They proved that Ruth not only had chosen to stay with her mother-in-law but also had chosen the God of Israel. Naomi's words about God had been heard and understood. Despite Naomi's backsliding, God had blessed her words. That itself was marvelous grace, an unmerited favor.

Has God ever used you to call others to Him even in a time of distance or backsliding? How did that make you feel?

Despite this encouraging experience, her arrival in Bethlehem had been a disappointment. The news of her return had traveled quickly. It stirred the entire city. "Have you heard the news?" the people had shouted to one another. "Naomi is back!"[12] Despite her long absence abroad, the

[10] Ruth 1:15
[11] Ruth 1:16
[12] Ruth 1:19, author's paraphrase.

people still remembered her. Was she not related to Boaz, their rich fellow citizen?

But the reactions of the people when they first greeted her had shown Naomi how much she had changed. "Can this be Naomi?" the women had asked in disbelief.[13] Through their eyes, she saw herself mirrored. She had become a woman with an inanimate face on which sorrow had etched deep furrows. Her personality had lost all color. Her name meant "pleasant," but clearly her joy had gone; and the people of Bethlehem knew it.

"Don't call me Naomi. Call me Mara," she had answered impulsively.[14] The name Mara meant "bitter," and that was the way she had felt at that moment. That was the name she wanted to be called. But her bitterness stemmed from self-pity, and self-pity usually blames someone else. This is also what had happened to Naomi. Her pent-up feelings of sorrow and despair had given way to an accusation against God. "The Almighty has made my life very bitter," she said. "I went away full, but the LORD has brought me back empty."[15]

Are you grappling with bitterness or self-pity in any areas of your life? Have you lashed out against God in your hurt? What are five things you can do to intentionally work to change your perspective?

---

[13] Ruth 1:19
[14] Ruth 1:20
[15] Ruth 1:20-21

She didn't say a word about the fact that Elimelech and she had moved away from God when they had traveled to Moab. At that moment, she had not yet realized that she had not returned empty. She now had a loving daughter-in-law who wanted to share her life.

From that moment on, however, her life had begun to change. As obviously as God's blessing had been absent in Moab, it became evident in Bethlehem.

She had often mused about the words that Moses, the Law-giver, had been given by God to say: "I am setting before you today a blessing and a curse—the blessing if you obey the commands of the Lord your God that I am giving you today; the curse if you disobey the commands of the Lord your God and turn from the way that I command you today by following other gods, which you have not known."[16]

Naomi had experienced God's blessing through Ruth, who from the beginning had cared for her like a daughter. She had also seen God's blessing through His leading. From the first moment, He had led them both toward Boaz, the man who would radically change their lives.

When Naomi became aware of God's dealings with them and suspected that He was giving Ruth the joy of a new marriage with Boaz, she said to Ruth, "My daughter, I must find a home for you, where you will be well provided for."[17]

Boaz was a rich landlord, but even more importantly, he was a man who feared the Lord. Once he fell in love with

[16] Deuteronomy 11:26-28
[17] Ruth 3:1

Ruth, he had shown no hesitancy to marry her. As a result of the marriage, little Obed now sat on Naomi's lap. Ruth, whose marriage with Mahlon had remained childless, now had been blessed by God with a child.

The child's movement stopped Naomi's musing about the past. The neighbor women all said, "A son has been born to Naomi." She smiled at the "grandson" who did not even have the slightest trace of her blood in his veins. This thought did not make her bitter. She didn't poison her pleasure with thoughts of what could have been. She didn't say that she would have been happier holding Mahlon and Ruth's child.

———————

What are some unhelpful thoughts of "what could have been" that you are allowing (or have allowed in the past) to poison what God has given you now? What are some specific pieces of Scripture you can use to combat those thoughts?

———————

Naomi accepted the facts. She opened her heart to Obed as if he were her own grandson. After all, he was the son of Ruth, who was more precious to her than seven sons. That in itself was complete happiness, and so she was grateful. According to Jewish law, on the other hand, she did have a grandson, for Obed was counted as the son of Mahlon.

Naomi's future was finally bright. Every thought about loneliness disappeared like snow before the sun. Ruth, for

GIEN KARSSEN || 89

whom she had lovingly cared, now did everything she could to bring her mother-in-law happiness. The grandmother took care of the child.

Naomi once more became the pleasant one, a person who gave and received love. The Mara period now lay behind her. "Praise be to the LORD," the neighbor women had said,[18] and these words stayed in her heart. God had been good to her despite hardships, sorrows, and her own failures.

How good had He been? She had no idea at this time that the sprawling child on her lap would become a special link in the history of her people and in the history of redemption. How could she even imagine that she was cherishing the grandfather of Israel's most beloved king, David? Only the future would reveal that with David the birth of the Messiah would come into sight. Naomi, who was mindful of the well-being of others, did not have the faintest idea that her life would be connected with the Savior of the world, Jesus Christ, who would come over a thousand years after her.

---

[18] Ruth 4:14

8

BATHSHEBA

A Powerless Woman to Whom God Gave a Voice

Therefore murder shall be a constant threat in your family
from this time on because you have insulted me by taking
Uriah's wife.

2 SAMUEL 12:10, TLB

READ

2 Samuel 11:1-17, 26-27

• • •

THE GLORIOUS FUTURE ABIGAIL SAW for David had already
been realized for a long time. After David had been king over
Judah for seven and a half years, he became the ruler over the
entire nation of Israel. During his rule he encountered quite
a few storms that affected him and his wives.[1] Despite these
difficulties, however, one fact remained the same. He was still
faithful toward God. David was a righteous king, treating
each of his subjects fairly.

---
[1] 1 Samuel 30:1-6

What positive things does the Bible say
about David (2 Samuel 5:10; Acts 13:22)?
What negative (2 Samuel 12:10; 1 Kings 15:5)?

Over and over again the Lord confirmed that He was with David. The name of the God of Israel became highly respected among the nations around Israel.

But there were signs of faithlessness. The rainy season that had stopped the war against the Ammonites was over, and General Joab and his army had returned to battle.[2] King David, however, did not march with his troops as he used to do. He stayed at home. He abdicated his leadership role and instead dwelt in idleness. This idleness was not good for him. The distraction and apathy opened the door for Satan to thrust temptation in the path of this man of God.[3] And so David took a walk one fateful evening in the spring. He could not sleep, and he got out of bed and walked outside. There, from the roof of his palace, he saw a woman named Bathsheba taking her bath on the flat roof of her house.

David, inactive and shirking his duties as Israel's king, proved to be easy prey for Satan's temptations. He had never, like Job, made a covenant with his eyes not to look with desire on other women.[4] He had never made a deliberate stand against the shameful sin of lust that becomes a destructive fire in the life of the man who commits it.

---

[2] 2 Samuel 11:1
[3] 1 Peter 5:8
[4] Job 31:1

Just like that fateful time in paradise—Satan is not very original—temptation again made use of the eyes. Like Eve,[5] David desired what his eyes saw. He did not renounce the desire immediately and radically, and so the evil could no longer be curbed.

How do you combat temptation? Knowing that Satan prowls around like a roaring lion, what are some specific ways you can guard your eyes and renounce sinful desires?

Bathsheba was an unusually beautiful woman. Her father, Eliam, was one of David's heroes. Her husband, Uriah, was a dedicated and courageous officer in the king's army who performed his services dutifully and conscientiously.

Scripture does not give us insight into Bathsheba's state of mind in all of this, but there is no reason to believe that she expected to be seen. Perhaps she had never previously seen a man on that section of the palace roof. Was not the king a military man who spent much of his time away from home?

The king's summons for her to come to him at the palace was very much in line with the behavior of Eastern monarchs, but this manner of behavior was unworthy of David, the man after God's heart. When the call from the royal court arrived, Bathsheba naturally went. As a subject, and as a woman in that culture, she had to obey. She was not

[5] Genesis 3:6

the instigator responsible for the dramatic events that were about to develop.

Bathsheba was in a powerless position. Perhaps she tried to call David to what God would have him do, as Abigail did,[6] or perhaps she feared for her life if she refused. Her situation could be compared to that of Joseph's, who was also in a position of powerlessness as a servant and went to prison after he courageously said, "How then could I do such a wicked thing and sin against God?"[7] But as a woman, she could have been forced even if she had tried to take a stand.

Study the story of David and Bathsheba in light of James 1:14-15. How did David's sin start?

In his sin against Bathsheba and Uriah—and ultimately against God—David, the man after God's heart, forever cast blame on his own name. He gave Israel's enemies a reason to slander God's name.[8] David insulted God a thousand years before Christ. Two thousand years after Christ, the floodlights of Hollywood would still mercilessly reveal the sin of David. The Bible doesn't cover anything up. It removes every doubt whether or not David was the father of Bathsheba's child. All the facts gradually came to light, and with those facts appeared the startling development of sin. What started with David's dereliction of duty toward his army developed

---

[6] 1 Samuel 25:23-31
[7] Genesis 39:9
[8] 2 Samuel 12:14

through deceitful lust—even after he had been told that Bathsheba was married—into murder.

These developments precisely followed the pattern about which James later warned.[9] David's lustful desire lured and enticed him and, because he yielded to it, resulted in death. Literal death came to at least five people.

Consider a time when your sin impacted other people. What did God teach you through that situation?

David's conscience proved to be so dulled that he didn't acknowledge the extent of his deeds until the prophet Nathan confronted him with them.[10] But by then over nine months had already passed. The man who had experienced a walk with God so intensely that he could say, "You, God, are my God, earnestly I seek you; I thirst for you, my whole being longs for you, in a dry and parched land where there is no water,"[11] kept silent all those months before his God. And because his perception of God was darkened, he also missed clear sight of himself.

Consistently choosing to live in sin dulls our conscience. When have you experienced this? How did God call you to repentance?

[9] James 1:14-15
[10] 2 Samuel 12:1-9
[11] Psalm 63:1

When Nathan placed David's sin before him without mentioning any names, the king pronounced the sentence of death for the delinquent without any hesitation.

David's sin started a chain reaction of death and sorrow, for "the thing David had done displeased the LORD."[12] It is striking that this sin was laid at David's feet alone. This again speaks to the weight of David's role and power in taking advantage of a powerless woman. Although according to the law of Moses he deserved to die,[13] God was gracious. David would remain alive after he confessed his sin, but the child he had conceived with Bathsheba would die.

There was, furthermore, a double curse on David's life. Because David had dishonored God by killing Uriah, the sword would never depart from his house.[14] He would also be punished for taking Uriah's wife; another man would publicly dishonor his wives.

These predictions were literally fulfilled. The little baby of David and Bathsheba died right away.[15] Uriah had been killed. Three of David's sons—Amnon,[16] Absalom,[17] and Adonijah[18]—died violent deaths. David's concubines were dishonored by one of his sons in the sight of all Israel.[19]

The Bible does not simply describe the deeds of men; it also proclaims the greatness of God and His infinite grace. After David realized and confessed that he had, first of all,

---

[12] 2 Samuel 11:27
[13] Leviticus 20:10
[14] 2 Samuel 12:10
[15] 2 Samuel 12:19
[16] 2 Samuel 13:28-30
[17] 2 Samuel 18:14
[18] 1 Kings 2:24-25
[19] 2 Samuel 16:22

sinned against God, he was freed from his burden of sin. He became happy because of his rediscovered fellowship with the Lord and expressed life's new meaning in a touching psalm of repentance.[20] His life gained a new dimension, which is seen in the jubilant opening lines of another psalm. "Blessed is the one whose transgressions are forgiven, whose sins are covered," he exclaimed. "Blessed is the one whose sin the LORD does not count against them and in whose spirit is no deceit."[21] David did not excuse himself; he did not minimize what he had done—to God and to Bathsheba and Uriah.

As a beautiful sign of God's grace, Bathsheba, once a power-less woman, was given a voice in the kingdom by becoming the mother of Solomon, who in due time would be a king known for his wisdom and riches. The prophet Nathan, whom God had chosen to announce His judgment, called the baby Jedidiah, which meant "loved by the LORD."[22]

Have you ever felt as though you didn't have a voice? How did God work in that situation? How did your relationship with God change because of your circumstances?

Bathsheba later acted as an intermediary through whom her son Solomon became an heir to the throne,[23] and she

---

[20] Psalm 51
[21] Psalm 32:1-2
[22] 2 Samuel 12:24-25
[23] 1 Kings 1:11-31

appears among the ancestors of the Savior of the world, Jesus Christ.[24]

The story of David and Bathsheba has become a monument that tells of the faithfulness of God. It stands as an encouragement for every human being who, like David, has confessed his sin and learned to live by grace. And for every person who feels powerless, we see the promise that God gives voice to those who are voiceless.

[24] Matthew 1:6

9
THE WIDOW
OF ZAREPHATH

A Woman Who Accepted the Challenge of Faith

Faith is not merely an act, but a series of acts. It is a maintained attitude of the heart, an unquestioned obedience. Faith must have a divine warrant upon which to rest, and it finds this in the promises of God.

J. OSWALD SANDERS, *MIGHTY FAITH*

READ

1 Kings 17:7-24

• • •

SHE LIVED IN THE LITTLE HARBOR TOWN OF ZAREPHATH between Tyre and Sidon in Phoenicia. Her husband was dead. She and her little son were near death as well, for there was a terrible drought in the land. There had been no rain for many days. The water supplies had been exhausted, and the land was incapable of producing any crops. Food supplies were running out and could not be replenished. The difficulties of daily living were mounting not only for this widow but for every other inhabitant of the country.

Have you ever experienced a situation in which you felt your "supplies"—whether emotional, physical, or spiritual—were running out? How did God provide during that time?

She had a little oil and flour left—just enough to prepare a final meal for herself and her child. After eating this, they could only wait for death. She went out to gather wood to prepare their last meal. When she arrived at the city gate she saw a man in a long, loose garment held together with a leather belt. She did not know him, for he was a stranger. He was Elijah, a prophet of Israel.

He called to her and asked her to bring a little water in a vessel for him to drink. She realized that he was a holy man. She could see that by his clothes. Though she had no water to spare, she felt she could not disappoint him. She must do what he requested. The God of Elijah was not her god. She was a heathen. But she had heard enough about the God of Israel to feel a deep respect and awe for Him. As she turned to go back home for the water, he said, "Bring me a morsel of bread in your hand."

How did you come to follow Christ? How has God caused your faith to grow through difficult situations? Reflect on specific experiences and how those impacted you.

She explained the situation to him, saying, "As the Lord your God lives, I don't have anything baked. All I have is a handful of meal and a little oil in a cruse. I am out gathering some sticks in order to prepare this for my son and myself so we may eat it, and die." She expected her somber story would convince him that, unfortunately, she could not comply with his request. But this was not the case. He replied, "Don't be afraid. Go and fix the meal as you have planned, but first make me a little cake and bring it to me. Then afterward make some for yourself and your son. For the Lord, the God of Israel, promises that the jar of meal will not run out and the cruse of oil will not fail until the Lord again sends rain upon the earth."[1]

Has God ever offered unexpected provision to you, through friendships, finances, etc.? How did that impact your relationship with Him?

She had never before had anything that couldn't run out. Personally she had never had any dealings with the God of Israel. Although this man spoke in the name of God, what guarantee did she have that he was sent by Him? She was willing to take the risk for herself, but she had to consider the life of her child. Her only child . . .

A great act of faith was being asked of this heathen woman. She was challenged to believe the word of a man when she didn't have any proof that he was even a servant of God. How could she trust him?

---

[1] 1 Kings 17:12-14, author's paraphrase

But she sensed an authority in the voice of the man. She decided to take the risk. And after she had served the prophet his meal, there was still flour and oil left over for her and her son!

This miracle repeated itself for many days. The experience was similar to God's continued provision of bread to the Israelites in the wilderness.[2] It continued to be a daily challenge of her faith. The supply was always of such scanty measure that she could not put any food aside and trust in it. She could trust only in the promise of God.

Have you ever experienced a time in life when God seemed to be providing only enough for each day, tangibly or intangibly? Looking back, do you think this developed your faith? Why or why not?

So every day an act of faith was required from her, faith in the word that was spoken. And daily she, her son, and Elijah experienced a miracle, for every day there was enough for all of them to eat. This continued for many days. Her faith became anchored in God.

Then something occurred that was impossible for her to understand. Elijah had come to live in her home, using the spare upper room. The author of Hebrews states that a person who is hospitable may lodge angels unaware.[3] This was her experience. The angel of death, busily at work during a

[2] Exodus 16
[3] Hebrews 13:2

time of famine, did not enter her door, and she did not fall victim to him.

Therefore, it was inconceivable to her that her son should suddenly become ill. Even before she had time to tell the prophet, her son died. She didn't understand! Why had God kept the child alive during the famine only to allow him to die now? Death was snatching his prey from an entirely different angle.

With the presence of the holy man of God in her house, she had come to realize that she was a sinful woman. Was this why her son had died? Did sin demand a penalty? She confronted the prophet with this question. She was desperate.

"Give me your son," Elijah said. He took the dead boy up to his room and put him on his own bed. Then he wrestled with God in prayer about the child. "O LORD my God, have You brought calamity to the widow with whom I board by slaying her son? Return this child's soul to him again," he begged, while stretching himself upon the child three times.[4] It seemed as if he wanted to transmit his life and the warmth of his body into the cold, still form of the boy. To Elijah's unspeakable joy, God answered his prayer. He saw life flowing back into the child. He returned the boy alive to his mother. The resurrection of the widow's small son is the first biblical record of a person being raised from death.

The widow had experienced a crisis in her faith. The miracle of the multiplication of the food had strengthened her faith in the prophet's mandate. His commission was true. He

---

[4] 1 Kings 17:20-21, author's paraphrase

did speak the Word of God. He could be trusted. But she had never expressed this clearly in words. She was so closely connected with the present drama, so captured by surprise and so shocked, that she was unable to realize that God was doing something wonderful for her.

Later, when the famine was over, she would look back and experience a double blessing, for she had not only experienced having her life prolonged day by day but had also witnessed a resurrection from the dead.

As a result of this experience, she made a clear statement of faith: "Now I know that you are a man of God, and that the words that you speak are true."[5] She would never again doubt the Word of God. The second test of faith was much more difficult than the first, but she came through, matured and enriched.

Deep suffering should stimulate greater faith. Such a faith, however, must first be tested for genuineness. God wants to know its value and, therefore, allows suffering. The faith that remains after the test of suffering is pure.[6]

---

1 Peter 1:6-7 says that faith is tried for its genuineness. Read 1 Kings 17:17-24 again, especially the last verse. How did the widow experience this, and how did she withstand the trial?

---

[5] 1 Kings 17:24, author's paraphrase
[6] 1 Peter 1:6-7; 4:12-13

Reflect on a time of suffering in your life. What do you believe that time revealed about your faith?

This woman learned that God puts a high reward on faith.[7] She developed sensitivity for the unseen yet very real world of faith. The testing that God put her through enabled her to understand the reality, assurance, and proof of His faithfulness.[8]

[7] Hebrews 11:6
[8] Hebrews 11:1-2

10
MARTHA OF BETHANY

A Woman Who Learned What Was Important

My prayer for you is that you may have still more love—a love
that is full of knowledge and wise insight. I want you to be
able always to recognise the highest and the best.

PHILIPPIANS 1:9-10, PH

READ

Luke 10:38-42; John 11:17-27, 32-44

• • •

MARTHA WAS TENSE. A moment ago thirteen guests, all men,
had dropped in unexpectedly. Jesus—the Master—and His
disciples stopped by on their way to Jerusalem, which was
just two miles down the road.

The visitors were not unknown guests. Jesus was a good
friend of Martha; her sister, Mary; and their brother, Lazarus.
Jesus sometimes arrived with His disciples late at night to
stay with them in Bethany.

Martha was grateful that the Master, who had no place
to lay His head,[1] felt at home with them. She was hospitable

---
[1] Matthew 8:20

and lovingly opened her home to others. She considered it an honor to please her guests.

You don't need a perfect home to welcome others—hospitality takes many forms. What is one intentional way you can show hospitality this week?

Martha wrestled with herself as she attended to the needs of the dusty and hungry men. It was not that her home was not spacious enough or that her pantry was poorly provided with food. She was rich enough. However, she was irritated because her sister, Mary, was not helping her serve.

Mary was totally absorbed as she listened to the Master. She eagerly drank in His every word. The uppermost questions in her mind were, "How can I enjoy Him the most? What can I learn?"

Martha was no less happy to have Jesus visit them than her sister, but she did not enjoy it as completely. Her thoughts were constantly occupied by details and secondary issues. That was why the greatness of the occasion escaped her. She was nervous. Irritated! And, as can be usual in such a situation, she found fault with the other person.

Even good things can prevent us from keeping Jesus as our first concern. What secondary issues tend to be primary in your thoughts?

Martha suffered from self-pity. "Lord," she interrupted, "don't You care that my sister has left me to serve alone?"[2]

Consider a time when you placed blame on another person and later felt convicted about your role in the situation. Why did you initially place blame? What did you learn from that decision?

Martha didn't seem to care that she was accusing her sister in the presence of her guests and that she was implicating Jesus in the accusation! And that was not all. She dared to order the Master to make Mary come and help her.

The voice of the Master, which had kept the listeners spellbound, stopped abruptly. "Martha, Martha," He said, "you worry and trouble yourself over so many things, but only one is necessary. Mary has chosen the right thing, and it should not be taken away from her."[3]

With those few words He implied much more. They contained a warning:

Martha, how can you mingle the primary and secondary issues in such a manner? How can you become lost in things of minor importance while I am in your home? Martha, don't you understand that I came in the first place to serve? Not to be served?[4] Don't you see that I am much more interested in you than in shelter and food? I do appreciate your hospitality, but

[2] Luke 10:40, author's paraphrase
[3] Luke 10:41-42, author's paraphrase
[4] Matthew 20:28

My first concern is for Martha, not the hostess. Martha, you are so efficient and wise—why must you do everything, even the smallest detail, by yourself? Don't you understand that I prefer a simple meal anyway? In My Kingdom priority is given to spiritual matters. Examine yourself. Know your own heart. Look at things from My point of view.

Mary doesn't need to receive correction; you do. But I say all this only because I love you.[5] Things of temporal value and worries about this life choke My Word[6] and darken your view of eternal matters. Also, Martha, be careful about judging someone else.[7] Leave that to Me instead.[8] Test yourself and judge your own heart.[9]

Consider a time when you received correction from the Lord—either through personal conviction or through the voice of someone He has placed in your life. How did that make you feel? What did God teach you through the correction?

The next meeting between Jesus and this family took place under extremely sad circumstances. Sickness and fear had entered the happy home. Lazarus was seriously ill. Without delay his sisters sent a message to Jesus, who was preaching on the other side of the Jordan River. All they said to Him was, "Lord, Your friend is very ill."

[5] Hebrews 12:5-6
[6] Mark 4:19
[7] Matthew 7:1,2
[8] 1 Corinthians 4:5
[9] 2 Corinthians 13:5

They expected Him to come right away. They knew when it would be possible for Him to arrive there. But Jesus stayed away—on purpose—and Lazarus died.

Have you ever felt frustrated that God didn't show up "on time" in a difficult situation? How did He eventually manifest Himself in that circumstance?

God would be glorified through this illness in a special way. Mary and Martha would rejoice not about their brother's healing but about his resurrection from the dead.

This was beyond their perception. Therefore, the sisters repeated many times a day, "If the Lord had been here, Lazarus would not have died."

Then, when Lazarus had been buried for four days and the house was full of comforting friends, Jesus arrived. Mary, overcome by sorrow, stayed at home, but Martha's character could not deny itself. How could she sit quietly at home when the Master was coming? Impossible! She went to meet Him and repeated what she and Mary had said so often: "This would not have happened, Lord, if You had been here."

Again, there was a tinge of accusation in her words to Jesus, but they were also an expression of faith and hope. She proved this when she added, "But I know that even now God will give You whatever You ask of Him."[10]

---

[10] John 11:21-22, author's paraphrase

All was not lost.

When He promised, "Your brother will be raised to life," Martha thought of the distant future. But Jesus confronted her with an overwhelming fact: "I am the resurrection and the life."

The resurrection didn't offer hope for the future only. It was a present reality. That reality was personified in the Man who was speaking to her. Not only did He give life, He was life Himself.

What do you think it means that resurrection
is both a present and a future reality?
How has Jesus caused resurrection in your life?
How has He manifested Himself as life itself?

Martha's answer was a remarkable confession of faith: "Yes, Lord! I do believe that You are the Messiah, the Son of God, who has come into the world."[11]

The question that so many had asked and that had brought such division was: "Is He the Christ or not?"[12] Martha had given a positive answer even though she could not imagine the implication of her testimony. The woman who had once struggled to make Christ first priority now expressed unwavering faith and trust in Him.

What happened next is very moving. Martha had called Mary. She arrived and greeted Jesus. They saw that Jesus was

[11] John 11:27, author's paraphrase
[12] Matthew 11:3; John 7:31, 41-43

deeply sorrowful. The words of Isaiah became reality: "In all their distress he too was distressed."[13]

The Son of God was not ashamed of His tears. He wept.

The sisters and all who had come to mourn saw it. Some said, "See how much He loved him." Others were critical, saying, "He opened the blind man's eyes, didn't He? Then why couldn't He keep Lazarus from dying?"[14]

Then Jesus' sufferings came to light. He would not only suffer in His own approaching death. In this holy moment, when He proved His victory over death, Jesus suffered in life. He had done that every day of His earthly existence. He had suffered from the misunderstanding of the people.[15] He had suffered from the unfaithfulness of His friends.[16]

At the grave, Martha again interrupted Him. When He gave the order to remove the stone from the grave, she thought it necessary to remind Him that Lazarus, having been in the grave for four days, would be in a state of decomposition.

"Didn't I tell you that you would see God's glory if you believed?" Jesus answered. A gentle reminder, an encouragement to rest in the belief she had so recently expressed.

In what areas of your life do you need encouragement to believe in who God is? What are three passages of Scripture that speak such encouragement to you?

---

[13] Isaiah 63:9
[14] John 11:36-37, author's paraphrase
[15] Mark 6:1-6
[16] Matthew 26:31-35; Luke 22:39-45

Upon His shout, "Lazarus, come out!" death released its prey. Lazarus stood before them, alive. They could touch him. Jesus, who had taken upon Himself the blame of insensitivity to the sorrow of His friends, now sealed His friendship with the people of Bethany with His life.

Now His freedom was limited. He needed to hide Himself in order not to fall into the hands of the Pharisees and chief priests prematurely.[17] In a few weeks He would die on the cross. He would die not only for the sins of Lazarus, Martha, and Mary, but also for the sins of the whole world.

Six days before Jesus' death, Martha served at a banquet given in His honor.[18] The story is told in few words. Martha had not stopped serving. She had not fallen from one extreme to another. She was a woman of striking character. The beautiful characteristics of hospitality and a willingness to serve were still evident. She was also a woman whose faith, with the death of Lazarus, had stood the test.

Martha was a courageous woman. She remained faithful to the Lord at a time when the Jews' hatred was the most vehement and would result in His death.

Jesus loved her. He extended to her the honor of His friendship. He who knew people understood that women like Martha can suffer needlessly simply because of themselves. He knew that a good, intelligent, energetic woman like her could easily stumble and get lost in matters of secondary importance. Women like Martha have a particular need for Jesus. He can keep them from dedicating their lives to the second best.

[17] John 11:53-54
[18] John 12:1-2

11

THE SAMARITAN WOMAN

A Woman Who Said Yes to Jesus

Christ led me to the experience of overwhelming Reality. . . .
It is impossible to express all that this means in the way of
liberation, space, joy.

WILHELMINA, FORMER QUEEN OF THE NETHERLANDS

READ

John 4:4-26, 39-42

• • •

RELUCTANTLY, THE WOMAN LIFTED the empty water pitcher
up to her shoulder and, under the scorching noonday sun,
set out along the dusty road from Sychar. She hated the very
idea of this journey, but she had no alternative. She was too
poor to pay a servant, and being a woman of bad reputation,
she didn't dare go to the well at a later hour when the air
would be cooler. She could not run the risk of meeting the
other villagers when they went to the well to draw their daily
ration of water.

She was an outcast without friends. This was a consequence

of the kind of life she was leading. And in a small village it was especially noticeable.

Have you ever felt like an outcast?
What did Jesus say to you during that time?

While still a long way away, she saw a Man sitting by the well. Even from that distance she could see that He was weary. As she approached, she saw by His dress and features that He was a Jew. She wondered what had brought this Man to this place. Jews had such a deep-rooted hatred of the Samaritans that they avoided Samaria at all costs. When traveling from Judea to Galilee, they usually made a wide detour around the country. "Samaritans," they would say, "have no part in life after death." And, "He who eats the bread of a Samaritan is like someone who eats pork." Nothing could be more contemptible.

Her amazement increased when the Man asked her a favor. He was unlike any other Man. Could it be His voice? He spoke with authority but was not dictatorial. Or was it His expression, His human interest?

She was uncomfortable, ill at ease in the presence of His forceful personality. It is understandable that she could not place Him as the Master, for not only did the Jews have nothing whatsoever to do with the Samaritans, but it was even forbidden for a Jewish man to talk to a woman on the street.

"It would be better that the Articles of the Law be burned than that their contents be revealed to a woman publicly," said their rabbis.

Why then did this Man seek to contact her—not only a Samaritan but a woman as well?

Jesus shows us our value and worth even when we view ourselves as unworthy. What is a lie that you're believing about your unworthiness right now or that you have believed in the past?

Jesus disregarded her confusion. He aroused her curiosity by speaking about living water. If she only knew who it was who was talking to her! The words "living water" struck her. That would be the answer to her problem. That would mean no more daily, dreaded journeys to draw water. She didn't realize that all the water in the world could not quench her thirst. A solution to her material problem was not the real answer. Her deepest need was in her soul.

How does Jesus quench your thirst for Him?

And that was just where Jesus was aiming. He wanted to make her conscious of the necessity of meeting this need. He had come to Samaria for this purpose.

She didn't understand Him. Engrossed as she was in her daily problems, she had neglected the needs of her soul. "Give me some of this water so that I will not be thirsty again," she said. "Then," she continued, "I will not need to come to this well every day."[1]

What daily problems are distracting
you from the needs of your soul?

His answer was a simple but most bewildering request: "Go, call your husband and come back."

Why do you think Jesus told her to
"Go, call your husband and come back"?

Your husband, your husband—but she had no lawful husband. It was frightening when this Man spoke these words, especially when the conversation had been progressing so favorably. She had had a lot of experience as far as men were concerned, but she could not lie to this One. "I don't have a husband," she retorted. "I am not married."

"That is correct," Jesus told her. "You have had five husbands, and you are not married to the man with whom you are now living."[2]

------
[1] John 4:15, author's paraphrase
[2] John 4:17-18, author's paraphrase

This was dreadful. Were there no secrets from this Man? Her life was like an open book to Him.[3] And yet He neither despised nor blamed her. How strange! He had, however, made her conscious of the sick spot in her life—sin. Furthermore, He proved that He could not give her the coveted living water until this sin had been removed. As a religious woman she was fully aware of the laws concerning adultery. So far, however, she had been able to justify her actions by excuses.

But that time was past. She now clearly saw that her life had been governed by sin. Sin that could not continue in the eyes of God. Sin that had to be condemned—forcefully.

What is a sin area that God is asking you to remove from your life?

"Sir, I can see that You are a prophet," was all she could say. Then she began to talk about religion—how its forms and controversies divided the people. Religion always proved to be an interesting topic, and very safe. One could spend endless hours in discussions, making long arguments in which one could completely hide true feelings.

Jesus stuck to the main subject of the conversation. He was not to be diverted from the purpose for which He had come. He showed her with a few words that religion was a matter not of form but of content. God was looking for

[3] Hebrews 4:13

people who would seek Him with all their hearts, who would want to serve Him totally. The only thing valuable in God's sight was faith. This was what He was telling her. He didn't speak with a stately "Truly, truly, I say . . ." as He had to the learned Nicodemus,[4] but simply said, "Woman, believe Me." The desired result was the same—a new birth.

A longing for the Messiah filled her heart. The Christ—He would clarify everything that was still dark and obscure. Right then the conversation reached its climax. Jesus assured her that her longing was fulfilled—the future could become the present, then and there.

"I am the Messiah." Christ was not a figure in the distant future. He was flesh and blood. He stood before her. What He had told no one else so plainly, He disclosed to her: "I am the Christ."

For her, only for her, He had come to the much-hated Samaria. For her He had bypassed Jewish rules and regulations. The messianic hour had come. The time for discrimination was past. There was a solution for racial hatred and religious controversy. All human beings, even the most sinful, could now come to God through Jesus on two conditions: First, they must acknowledge their sin[5] and confess it.[6] They must acknowledge that they could not exist before a righteous God, for He is holy. Second, they must rely on Jesus Christ—that is, believe in Him. He is the Mediator between

---

[4] John 3:5, NASB
[5] Romans 3:23
[6] Romans 10:9-10

God and humans.[7] He bridged the gap that sin had made between man and God.

In a split second she saw it all very clearly. She was sinful, horrible, contemptible. He was full of love and understanding—forgiving. She understood that this was the reason He sought her. She received Him into her heart. She said yes to Jesus Christ.

The woman with a broken, battered past was inwardly free. Free from the penalty of sin and therefore, in God's sight, free from the stain of the past. People's criticism would no longer need to hurt her. From now on she could look people freely in the eye—unashamed. He who judged people, not by their outward appearance but according to their heart, had declared her free. How then could people accuse her?

Do you still feel accused for past sin? How can this passage help you find freedom in Christ?

The solution to her problems was total—both spiritual and material. The source of living water had cleansed her, quenched her thirst, and brought her a happiness she had never thought possible.

She was certainly not going to keep this to herself. She forgot why she had come to the well. There was something more important at stake. She hurried back to the village to spread

---
[7] John 14:6

the wonderful news that the Messiah had come. Sin could be forgiven. She must tell the people this—immediately!

She spoke to the people with the simple directness and freedom of one who has been in the presence of God, telling them of her experience.

"Come with me," she begged, "and meet the Man who knew my whole past. He surely must be the Christ."[8]

Her shyness was gone. She spoke about her disreputable past without hesitation or fear. It was remarkable that this past life, of which she had been so ashamed, should become the link with the happy present.

Our pasts are a part of our testimony of Christ's grace. What story has God given you to share with those around you?

The people, seeing the change in her, hurried from the village to Jacob's well. There they met the Messiah. Jesus did for them what He had done for the woman. He set them free. He gave them new life—eternal life.

They were impressed and begged Him to stay longer. So He did. Even more people came to listen to Him, and more—and more.

They told the woman, "We believe not because of what you have said, but because we have heard Him ourselves. We are personally convinced that He is the Savior of the world."[9]

[8] John 4:39, author's paraphrase
[9] John 4:42, author's paraphrase

And that was good. Christ should have the attention, not the woman. Christ should get the glory. She was only a finger pointing toward Him.

Four years passed. The earth and the heavens had been covered with a thick darkness on the day when the innocent Jesus of Nazareth, both God and Man, was crucified.

After the crucifixion, the angels proclaimed His resurrection—and forty days later at His ascension, they proclaimed His future return to earth. Some days later the Holy Spirit descended from heaven—first on individuals, then on large crowds. Thousands and thousands of people experienced the beginning of a new life.

Then the awful persecution of the new believers arrived. Satan didn't—and doesn't—release his prey easily. When it became too dangerous for the Christians to remain in Jerusalem, some fled to Samaria.

A great evangelistic movement began in Samaria. It was so successful that an evangelist was needed to further the ministry. When Philip came and preached to great crowds, many turned to Christ. Again there was happiness in the town, culminating in the outpouring of the Holy Spirit.[10] Differences between Jews and Samaritans were abolished forever. The gospel was poured out upon the world. The Good News was spreading from town to town. And because of her willingness to share, the evangelistic movement in Samaria will forever be associated with a woman.

The story of the Samaritan woman plainly illustrates

---

[10] Acts 8:1-17

that, although a person without Christ is a mission field, at the moment of receiving Him this same person becomes a missionary—a missionary for Him by His grace. The entering of God's Son into a person's life makes the big difference.

12

SALOME

A Mother Who Thought to Ask the Best for Her Children

Salome was ambitious for her sons, and ambition is
commendable when it is in full agreement with the mind
and purpose of God. Ambition, when divinely directed,
can lead to the heights of honor but when selfishly pursued
can cast one down to the depths of degradation.

HERBERT LOCKYER, *ALL THE WOMEN OF THE BIBLE*

READ

Matthew 20:17-28

• • •

SALOME, THE MOTHER OF JOHN AND JAMES,[1] resolutely took
a few steps forward. Her sons followed her. She did not care
that she would interrupt Jesus. She did not wait till He had
finished talking. Salome had something on her heart to ask
the Master—something that could not wait.

It was nearly Passover, and Jesus and His disciples were
once again making the trip from Galilee to Judea. An increas-
ing number of people had flocked together around them to
go up to Jerusalem to celebrate the Feast of Passover. Among

[1] Matthew 27:56; Mark 15:40

them were the sick, the lame, and the blind—people who wanted Jesus to heal them.

The long journey through the countryside and across the Jordan River finally was finished. Then the group reached Jericho. The final miles that still separated them from Jerusalem could not be underestimated. The heaviest part of the trip—the climb over the steep and barren Judean hills—still lay ahead of them.

On the surface there did not seem to be much difference between this journey and the previous ones. But the disciples of Jesus knew better. The shadows of the Master's future suffering darkened His life, disturbing Salome's thoughts and those of His other friends.

The words that Jesus had spoken just before the small group left Galilee came to mind over and over again.

"I am going to be betrayed into the power of those who will kill Me," He had said.[2] That statement had caused them sorrow, since they now understood that He soon would part from them.

Only a few moments ago, He had again repeated those words and elaborated on them. Leaving the crowds alone for a brief while, He pulled His disciples aside.

"As you see," He said to them, "we are on our way to Jerusalem. The Son of Man is to be delivered into the hands of men, and they will kill Him, and He will be raised on the third day."[3]

[2] Matthew 17:22-23, TLB
[3] Matthew 20:18-19, author's paraphrase.

These were astounding words. They revealed that Jesus would be rejected by the very people He came to save.[4] Although the religious leaders of the Jews would sentence Him to death, their decision would not cool down their hatred for Him. Before He died, they would mock Him, humiliate Him, and try to make a fool out of Him. The Man who had done only good would be openly executed like a common criminal.

Immediately preceding this terrible event, Jesus desired His fellow travelers to share His anguish. Were not His best friends—Peter, John, and James—among them, as well as Salome and the other women who had so faithfully served Him? Few people were closer to Him and knew Him any better. They would share His feelings, His sorrow.

Salome was the first and only person to respond to Jesus' words. Her voice sounded serious, but what she was saying had nothing to do with the Master. Her words had no real connection to His statements. Mother Salome showed no compassion toward the Savior and His approaching sufferings. She thought only of herself and her boys.

---

*Have you ever been guilty of placing
your own feelings and concerns
higher than what God desires?
How did that decision manifest itself?*

---

[4] John 1:11

When John the Baptist had started preaching over three years before Jesus did, the sons of Zebedee initially had joined him. Later, when Jesus had walked along the Sea of Galilee and called them, they had left their work and immediately followed Him.[5]

My sons may have an impetuous nature, and sometimes show insensitivity of character, Salome thought, *but they are, in fact, spiritual men. I understand why the other disciples have given them the surname "sons of thunder,"*[6] *yet their hearts are open toward the things of God.*

That was the reason why she and her husband, Zebedee, had not kept John and James from their intention to follow the Master. They had let their sons go without grumbling, without asking preference for their own interests.

**How do you respond when your plans
are disrupted by something you or
someone else senses God is asking?**

Zebedee had a prosperous fishing business, and his own sons could hardly be spared. They formed the hub around which much of the work centered. When the sons left, the business became much more dependent on the other workers, which was not advantageous.

Yet as parents, Salome and Zebedee had given this sacrifice gladly. They were happy that James and John—whom

[5] Mark 1:19-20
[6] Mark 3:17

they had given God-fearing educations—had reacted so positively. Deep in their hearts they were grateful that their sons were interested in God and were not eager to become rich.

It was a privilege for James and John—and their parents, indirectly—to be chosen as disciples of the Nazarene. The parents' gratitude had increased when they saw that John, who had a special place in Jesus' heart, gradually became His best friend.

These thoughts must have been in Salome's mind. For that reason she began to worry. After Jesus' repeated announcement of His suffering, the troubles that would result began to fill Salome's thinking.

What will happen to my boys when the Master is gone? Salome asked herself. *They have built their hopes on Him. Their futures are dependent on Him.*

Reflect on a time when you made a decision out of fear. What was the result?

In her thoughts Salome repeated Jesus' words. Then she realized that He had not only spoken of dying; He had also mentioned the resurrection.

That's it! Salome thought, relieved. *Jesus' final destination is not death. He will rise from the dead and set up His kingdom. Soon He will rule over His people as king.*

Now she knew what she had to do. Right away, she had to

make sure that her sons' future was assured. And who could better speak up for children than their mother?

For that matter, did not she herself have rights? Hadn't she sacrificially given of her life to the Master? Hadn't she shared the inconvenience of wandering about the countryside? Hadn't she given to Him of her time and possessions?

Have you ever felt like you deserve something from God because of what you've done? What skewed understanding of yourself and God is at the root of this perspective?

She quickly took a few steps forward. Then she knelt down before the Master to show her respect.

"What is your request?" Jesus asked kindly.[7]

Without further introduction, she told Him what she wanted. Her words gave vent to her train of thought. "Promise that my two sons may be sitting next to You in Your kingdom," she begged, "one at Your right hand, the other at Your left."[8]

Do you understand Salome's motives? What would you have done in her position?

[7] Matthew 20:21, author's paraphrase
[8] Matthew 20:21, author's paraphrase

Salome said what she had intended to say. Didn't it strike her that these words would sound harsh and egotistical in the Master's ears? Didn't she realize that He painfully experienced the absence of her love? Did she, even in part, sense how poorly she had responded to the situation in this moment? Was she aware of how small-minded her request was, compared to the greatness of the suffering that awaited the Master? The innocent Son of God was about to die, and the only thing Salome could think about was the future of her sons.

While the Son of God as a man stood staring in the face of death, longing for understanding and compassion, Salome only harbored feelings of motherly pride.

It is not clear whether Salome spoke for herself or if she was also the mouthpiece of her sons.[9] But even if the latter were true, it did not place her in a better light. It did not decrease her responsibility. On the contrary, her question revealed that she had missed the opportunity to correct them.

Jesus' other friends didn't come out any better. A short while later all the other disciples became furious over the requests of John and James. They did not react angrily because they knew that this request of their two fellow disciples had been painful to Jesus. Instead, they felt insulted for themselves—passed by. Now it was utterly clear how important James and John thought they were. Who were they to consider themselves so much more prominent than the rest?

---

[9] Mark 10:35-45

Consider Salome's actions and the response of the disciples in the context of Philippians 2:3. Why does self-importance have no place in the Kingdom of God?

Salome's words were heartless toward Christ, but they also showed little feeling for the mothers of His other disciples.

Why, the other women might well have been asking themselves, *should the sons of Zebedee be privileged again? Isn't it time that others—our sons—should be coming to the front? Haven't Peter and Andrew and the other disciples left everything as well? Haven't they also followed the Master?*[10]

Despite Salome's motherly pride, Jesus didn't rebuke her. The Son of Man standing before her was also God, able to probe into the deepest corners of a human heart. He not only recognized her selfish and negative traits but also saw more. He discerned her thoughts and desires. Her entire inner being lay open and bare before Him. He read her heart like a book.

No doubt it was frightening, but it was also encouraging. No one but the Creator of a mother's heart knows how her heart—with every fiber of its being—is attached to the child to whom she has given birth. He understood how vulnerable mothers are in this world, even in their relationships to God. He realized how easily a small child can come between

---
[10] Matthew 19:27

its mother and Himself. He saw the daily struggle mothers have gone through in this regard. Christian mothers are not exempt from such feelings.

So the Master didn't reprimand Salome. He understood and forgave. He knew that, next to her shortcomings, Salome had faith. She believed in His future, even though her view was humanly shortsighted and thus wrong. Jesus tasted her love through her desire to ensure that her sons would always stay close to Him.

It is valuable for every mother to consider Salome's request for her sons carefully, especially those mothers who—though they are aware of their human shortcomings and limitations—love the Lord deeply and are seeking the best for their children. They can learn many principles from this passage, especially in the area of prayer. Mothers must learn not to be too hasty in their prayers for their children. They must pray unselfishly and thoughtfully.

But there is also great encouragement connected with the story of Salome. God knows what is really best for a child, and He wants to provide it, even when the mother asks for the wrong thing. Instead of denying Salome's request, Jesus corrected it. Although at that moment she didn't recognize it, the answer to her prayer would come in an entirely different way from what she had expected.

Salome didn't know what she was asking. Thinking along human standards, she considered honor and reputation to be exceptionally great favors. Jesus, however, was led by godly thinking. The greatest honor in heaven was reserved for people who suffered because of their faith.

So His understanding response, addressed to John and James, went right over Salome's head: "Can you drink the cup I am going to drink?"[11]

The Lord Jesus was about to establish a heavenly kingdom instead of an earthly kingdom. The seats of honor in that kingdom would be allocated by God—His Father—and not by Him. The gate to that kingdom hinged upon suffering, the suffering of the Son of God.

How bitter His suffering was; every drop from His cup of suffering was mixed with gall. Salome experienced Jesus' suffering a few days later when she stood at the foot of His cross. Accompanied by His mother and several other women, she experienced parts of that suffering with Him. She was there when He shouted in agony of spirit: "My God, My God, why have you forsaken Me?"[12]

This heart-cry was directed to His Father in heaven, who at the beginning of Jesus' earthly ministry had said to Him: "You are my Son, whom I love; with you I am well pleased."[13]

The Lord's kingdom was founded on suffering and obedience. Salome's sons would get a place in that kingdom. But they had to enter it in the same way in which the Master would. He, the pioneer of salvation, would suffer heavily in order to bring many sons to glory.[14] He would hand out suffering as a favor, as a privilege, as a grace.

[11] Matthew 20:22
[12] Matthew 27:46
[13] Mark 1:11
[14] Hebrews 2:10

*The idea of suffering as a grace feels backward
to us. In what ways has God used suffering
to create eternal riches in your life?*

The most sparkling crown a person can wear is forged not by respect and honor but by unconditional obedience. The Bible states that the Son of God learned obedience in the school of suffering.[15] For His servants, there is no other way. Their measure of suffering—if undergone in the name of Christ—destines their future joy in glory.[16]

James and John already had an ample part in that suffering. But happily their pain was still hidden from their mother. Salome requested exceptional privileges for her sons and received them, expressed in suffering rather than a show of honor and glory.

Was Salome still alive when her son James, the first of the apostles to be martyred, was killed by the next king, Herod Agrippa I?[17] She never knew that her other son, John, was exiled at the end of his life for the sake of the gospel.[18]

James and John would not dominate the surroundings of an earthly king. But later, in heaven, they would radiate with martyrs' crowns because of the sufferings they went through in the name of Christ.

At the cross, Salome was treated exceptionally well. Jesus

---

[15] Hebrews 5:8
[16] 1 Peter 4:12-13
[17] Acts 12:1-2
[18] Revelation 1:9

appointed her son, John, to take care of His own mother.[19] The Savior granted to the disciple whom He loved above the others the honor to serve. Serving, like suffering, is a pillar on which the everlasting kingdom of God is being constructed. In this way, the principles of the Kingdom of God are diametrically opposed to those of earthly rulers.

Jesus brought this lesson to the attention of the women and His disciples that day at Jericho. His disciples should desire to impress through service rather than through domination. The people who are willing to be the least on earth will be counted the highest in heaven.

---

[19] John 19:25-27

About the Author

GIEN KARSSEN was raised in a Christian home and became a Christian at the age of twelve as a result of the influence of her parents' lives and training. After she had been married only six weeks, the Nazis interned her husband in a concentration camp, where he died. Just before his death he inscribed Luke 9:62 in his diary: "But Jesus said to him, 'No one, after putting his hand to the plow and looking back, is fit for the kingdom of God'" (NASB). This verse challenged Gien and gave purpose and direction to her life. Using this Scripture as a basis, she found it easier to face difficulties, cancel her own desires, and want God's will only.

She met Dawson Trotman, founder of The Navigators, in 1948 in Doorn, Holland. She started the Navigator ministry there by translating The Navigators' *Topical Memory System* into Dutch and handling all the enrollments. Over the years she worked in many capacities with The Navigators. Women who have been personally helped by Gien Karssen can be found on almost every continent of the globe.

Gien was a popular speaker, Bible study leader, and trainer, as well as a freelance writer for Christian periodicals in Europe. The original edition of *Her Name Is Woman* (Book 1) was her first book and the first book ever published by NavPress. She also wrote *Beside Still Waters* and *The Man Who Was Different.*

Begin One of the Greatest
Journeys with This Series!

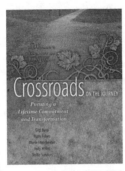

978-1-60006-786-0
$12.99

978-1-60006-785-3
$12.99

978-1-63146-538-3
$13.99

The series A WOMAN'S JOURNEY OF DISCIPLESHIP will take you deep
into a relationship with Christ. Throughout this journey,
you'll be introduced to basic spiritual disciplines, learn to
walk with Christ daily, make decisions using Scripture, and
discover the value of discipling other women to walk the
same journey.

Available everywhere books are sold
or online at NavPress.com.
1-855-277-9400

Become the Woman God Created You to Be.

Becoming a Woman of Simplicity
978-1-60006-663-4 | DVD 978-1-61521-821-9

What does it mean to enter into God's rest? Can women today do that, with multitasking, constant communication, and others clamoring for attention? Bestselling author Cynthia Heald helps you quiet the chaos and find true rest for your soul.

Becoming a Woman of Grace
978-1-61521-022-0

This inspirational study guides you on a life-transforming journey into the boundless riches of God's grace. You will explore the many ways in which God's grace enriches your Christian walk and discover how to know His grace more fully.

Becoming a Woman Who Loves
978-1-61521-023-7

In *Becoming a Woman Who Loves*, you'll explore the incredible nature of Christlike love and how God empowers us to love as Jesus loved.

Becoming a Woman of Faith
978-1-61521-021-3

This book will strengthen and encourage you as Cynthia shares candidly from her own faith journey. You'll see yourself in her personal struggles to walk in faith and trust, and you'll learn and grow from her special insights from God's Word.

Becoming a Woman of Strength
978-1-61521-620-8 | DVD 978-1-61747-902-1

We constantly encounter struggles and hardships of all kinds in our lives, but we can respond to them in our own weakness or with God's strength. This Bible study will encourage you to depend upon the strength of the Lord by seeking, waiting, serving, praying, and persevering in Him.

Becoming a Woman of Excellence
978-1-57683-832-7

Society beckons us to succeed — to achieve excellence in our appearance, our earning power, our family life. God Himself also beckons us to be women of excellence. But what exactly is He asking? In this motivational Bible study, you will discover what you should be striving for as you look to God's excellence as a model.

Becoming a Woman of Freedom
978-1-57683-829-7

Is your Christian life weighing you down? Get your second wind to identify and lay aside those burdens that make you feel "stuck." With challenging insights and thought-provoking quotations from classic thinkers and writers, *Becoming a Woman of Freedom* will help you develop the actions and attitudes you need to finish the race with strength.

Becoming a Woman of Prayer
978-1-57683-830-3

In *Becoming a Woman of Prayer*, you will be encouraged to respond to God's invitation to deeper intimacy with Him. Prayer is an opportunity for us to respond to His invitation to intimacy by calling, crying, and singing to Him. This guide shows us how to become women of prayer.

Becoming a Woman of Purpose
978-1-57683-831-0

As you grow toward genuine peace and fulfillment, you'll learn the joy of loving God and others, waiting on Him with hope, trusting Him through suffering, serving Him with reverent fear, and fulfilling His purposes.

Becoming a Woman Whose God Is Enough
978-1-61291-634-7

God desires to bless you with His fullness and to teach you to depend on Him completely. Learn to turn from worldly satisfactions to a life of contentment, from selfishness to humility, and from unbelief to rich fellowship with God.

Available wherever books are sold.

A NavPress resource published in alliance
with Tyndale House Publishers, Inc.   CP0795

Women of the Bible You Can Relate To

Believers

Jochebed	Elizabeth
Hannah	Anna
Rahab	The Poor Widow
The Jewish Maid	Mary of Jerusalem
Ruth	Tabitha
Mary	Lois and Eunice

Leaders

Miriam	Esther
Deborah	Mary of Bethany
Abigail	Mary Magdalene
The Queen of Sheba	Lydia
Huldah	Priscilla
The Shunammite	Phoebe

Learners

Eve	Naomi
Sarah	Bathsheba
Rebekah	The Widow of Zarephath
Leah	Martha of Bethany
Dinah	The Samaritan Woman
Tamar	Salome

Wanderers

Hagar	Job's Wife
Lot's Wife	Orpah
Rachel	Michal
Potiphar's Wife	Jezebel
Delilah	Herodias
Peninnah	Sapphira

Gien Karssen's vivid storytelling and deep insights will immerse you in the lives of these women. As you grapple with God's role in each woman's life, you will be inspired to live your own life wholeheartedly for God.

The Her Name Is Woman series is a favorite guide for Bible studies and small groups, with relevant Scripture passages and Bible study questions.

Available everywhere books are sold or online at NavPress.com.
1-855-277-9400

CP0927